# IOWA STATE PARKS

# Iowa Parks Foundation Centennial Celebration Committee

Mark Ackelson
Ann Raisch
Gerry Schnepf
Kevin Szcodronski

The Iowa Parks Foundation works to strengthen connections between Iowans and their parks through special initiatives that promote greater park use and partnerships that take a regional approach to planning, operations, and maintenance. *More people in more parks more of the time.*

# IOWA STATE PARKS

*A Century of Stewardship, 1920–2020*

BY REBECCA CONARD
PHOTO EDITORS ANGELA CORIO AND JIM SCHEFFLER

Iowa Parks Foundation, Des Moines, Iowa

Iowa Parks Foundation, Des Moines, Iowa
Copyright © 2020 by the Iowa Parks Foundation
Printed in Canada
ISBN 978-1-60938-713-6 (pbk)

Book design and typesetting by
Business Publications Corporation, Inc.

Cataloging-in-Publication data is on file at the Library of Congress.

The historic photos on pages 264 and 265 are from
the collection of Hank Zaletel.

MIX
Paper from
responsible sources
FSC® C016245

Dedicated to the conservationists and park advocates who created Iowa's state park system. May their legacy inspire another century of stewardship.

# Contents

**Foreword** *by Gerald F. Schnepf*..............................................................................................................xiii

**Acknowledgments**..........................................................................................................................................xv

**Navigating This Book**................................................................................................................................xvii

**A Brief History of Iowa's State Park System** *by Rebecca Conard*........................................................1

**Geological Foundations** *by Jean C. Prior*..............................................................................................7

**Ecosystems of Iowa's Parks and Preserves** *by Cornelia F. Mutel*....................................................15

**Biodiversity, Conservation, and the Land Ethic** *by John Pearson*....................................................19

**Archaeology of Iowa's State Parks and Preserves** *by William E. Whittaker*....................................25

**The Landscape Architectural Design of Iowa's State Parks** *by Heidi Hohmann*...........................29

**State Parks and State Recreation Areas**..................................................................................................37

      Ambrose A. Call State Park......................................................................................................42

      Backbone State Park...................................................................................................................44

      Badger Creek State Recreation Area.......................................................................................48

      Banner Lakes at Summerset State Park....................................................................................50

      Beeds Lake State Park................................................................................................................52

      Bellevue State Park.....................................................................................................................54

      Big Creek State Park..................................................................................................................56

      Black Hawk State Park...............................................................................................................58

      Bobwhite State Park...................................................................................................................60

      Browns Lake–Bigelow Park.......................................................................................................62

Brushy Creek State Recreation Area and State Preserve .......................................................................64

Cedar Rock State Park ...........................................................................................................................66

Clear Lake State Park | McIntosh Woods State Park ...........................................................................68

Cold Springs State Park .........................................................................................................................70

Crystal Lake State Park ..........................................................................................................................72

Dolliver Memorial State Park ...............................................................................................................74

Eagle Lake State Park .............................................................................................................................76

Echo Valley State Park ...........................................................................................................................78

Elk Rock State Park ................................................................................................................................80

Fort Defiance State Park ........................................................................................................................82

Frank A. Gotch State Park .....................................................................................................................84

Galland School ........................................................................................................................................86

Geode State Park .....................................................................................................................................88

George Wyth Memorial State Park ........................................................................................................90

Green Valley State Park ..........................................................................................................................92

Heery Woods State Park .........................................................................................................................94

Honey Creek State Park | Honey Creek Resort State Park ..................................................................96

Iowa Great Lakes Region: Elinor Bedell State Park, Emerson Bay State Recreation Area,
    Gull Point State Park, Lower Gar State Recreation Area, Marble Beach State Recreation Area,
    Mini-Wakan State Park, Pikes Point State Park, Pillsbury Point State Park, Templar State Recreation
    Area, Trappers Bay State Park ..........................................................................................................98

Kearny State Park ..................................................................................................................................102

Lacey-Keosauqua State Park ................................................................................................................104

Lake Ahquabi State Park ......................................................................................................................106

Lake Anita State Park ...........................................................................................................................108

Lake Cornelia State Park ......................................................................................................................110

Lake Darling State Park ........................................................................................................................112

Lake Keomah State Park .......................................................................................................................114

Lake Macbride State Park .....................................................................................................................116

Lake Manawa State Park .......................................................................................................................118

Lake Odessa Campground .................................................................................................................. 120

Lake of Three Fires State Park ........................................................................................................... 122

Lake Wapello State Park ..................................................................................................................... 124

Ledges State Park ................................................................................................................................. 126

Lewis and Clark State Park ................................................................................................................. 128

Maquoketa Caves State Park .............................................................................................................. 130

Margo Frankel Woods State Park ...................................................................................................... 132

Mines of Spain State Recreation Area | Catfish Creek State Preserve ....................................... 134

Nine Eagles State Park ........................................................................................................................ 138

Oak Grove State Park .......................................................................................................................... 140

Okamanpedan State Park .................................................................................................................... 142

Palisades-Kepler State Park | Palisades-Dows State Preserve ..................................................... 144

Pammel State Park ............................................................................................................................... 146

Pikes Peak State Park .......................................................................................................................... 148

Pilot Knob State Park | Pilot Knob State Preserve ......................................................................... 150

Pine Lake State Park ............................................................................................................................ 152

Pleasant Creek State Recreation Area .............................................................................................. 154

Prairie Rose State Park ........................................................................................................................ 156

Preparation Canyon State Park .......................................................................................................... 158

Red Haw State Park ............................................................................................................................. 160

Rice Lake State Park ............................................................................................................................ 162

Rock Creek State Park ......................................................................................................................... 164

Sharon Bluffs State Park ..................................................................................................................... 166

Springbrook State Park ....................................................................................................................... 168

Stone State Park | Mount Talbot State Preserve ............................................................................ 170

Swan Lake State Park ........................................................................................................................... 172

Twin Lakes State Park .......................................................................................................................... 174

Union Grove State Park ....................................................................................................................... 176

Viking Lake State Park ......................................................................................................................... 178

Volga River State Recreation Area .................................................................................................... 180

Walnut Woods State Park ........................................................................................................... 182

Wapsipinicon State Park ........................................................................................................... 184

Waubonsie State Park ............................................................................................................... 186

Wildcat Den State Park | Fairport State Recreation Area ......................................................... 188

Wilson Island State Recreation Area ........................................................................................ 190

## State Preserves ........................................................................................................... 193

Ames High Prairie State Preserve ............................................................................................ 198

Anderson Prairie State Preserve .............................................................................................. 199

Behrens Ponds and Woodland State Preserve .......................................................................... 200

Bixby State Preserve ................................................................................................................ 201

Bluffton Fir Stand State Preserve ............................................................................................ 202

Brush Creek Canyon State Preserve ........................................................................................ 203

Cayler Prairie State Preserve ................................................................................................... 204

Cedar Bluffs Natural Area and State Preserve ......................................................................... 205

Cedar Hills Sand Prairie State Preserve .................................................................................. 206

Cheever Lake State Preserve .................................................................................................... 208

Dinesen Prairie State Preserve ................................................................................................ 209

Doolittle Prairie State Preserve ............................................................................................... 210

Fallen Rock State Preserve ...................................................................................................... 211

Fish Farm Mounds State Preserve ........................................................................................... 212

Five Ridge Prairie State Preserve ............................................................................................ 213

Fort Atkinson State Preserve | Saint James Lutheran Church State Preserve ........................... 214

Fossil and Prairie Park State Preserve ..................................................................................... 216

Freda Haffner Kettlehole State Preserve .................................................................................. 217

Gitchie Manitou State Preserve ............................................................................................... 218

Glenwood Archaeological State Preserve ................................................................................. 220

Hayden Prairie State Preserve ................................................................................................. 222

Kalsow Prairie State Preserve .................................................................................................. 224

Malanaphy Springs State Preserve ........................................................................................... 225

Malchow Mounds State Preserve .................................................................................................................... 226

Manikowski Prairie State Preserve ................................................................................................................ 227

Marietta Sand Prairie State Preserve ........................................................................................................... 228

Merritt Forest State Preserve ........................................................................................................................ 229

Mossy Glen State Preserve ............................................................................................................................. 230

Sheeder Prairie State Preserve ...................................................................................................................... 231

Silver Lake Fen State Preserve ...................................................................................................................... 232

Steele Prairie State Preserve ......................................................................................................................... 233

Sylvan Runkel State Preserve ........................................................................................................................ 234

Toolesboro Mounds State Preserve ............................................................................................................... 236

Turin Loess Hills State Preserve ................................................................................................................... 237

Turkey River Mounds State Preserve ........................................................................................................... 238

Vincent Bluff State Preserve .......................................................................................................................... 240

White Pine Hollow State Preserve ................................................................................................................ 241

Williams Prairie State Preserve ..................................................................................................................... 242

Woodman Hollow State Preserve .................................................................................................................. 243


**State Forests** .................................................................................................................................................. 245

Loess Hills State Forest .................................................................................................................................. 248

Shimek State Forest ........................................................................................................................................ 250

Stephens State Forest ..................................................................................................................................... 252

Yellow River State Forest .............................................................................................................................. 254


**Further Reading** ........................................................................................................................................... 257

**Notes on Contributors** .............................................................................................................................. 261

**Index to Photographers** ........................................................................................................................... 263

# Foreword

**BY GERALD F. SCHNEPF**
— FOUNDING EXECUTIVE, IOWA NATURAL HERITAGE FOUNDATION
AND KEEP IOWA BEAUTIFUL

There's a special place in my memory for my childhood on the farm. Days were filled with chores, caring for livestock, maintaining buildings and machinery, producing crops, and helping tend the garden that produced generously for our family throughout the summer and whose bounty we preserved for the winter months.

In the bustle of daily life, it is the quiet time I consider fondly. A grove just north of our house helped me escape from chores and gave me the chance for the exploration young hearts need. I was Buck Rogers or the Lone Ranger on some days and Gene Autry or Tarzan on other days in the solace of that natural space. It afforded me the opportunity to be imaginative and creative.

Where do we find those special places today? With changes in our landscape, these groves of our youth have shrunk to make way for development. Thanks to forward-thinking folks, some of these unique places were saved by the creation of state parks and preserves across Iowa. For thousands of Iowans and visitors to our state, Iowa's state park system is a treasure trove of natural beauty, exploration, and tranquility. These parks and preserves often contain the key examples of our natural world and, in some instances, the heritage of our culture.

These Iowa state park jewels allow us to escape from the pressures of everyday life, to breathe in the natural beauty, in both the sounds and the silence. They reflect the spirit of our country. Whether they soothe the mind or challenge the body with recreation, Iowa's state parks allow us to play, pretend, explore, and refresh our souls. They are symbols of our conscience and how we feel about our state.

This country and Iowa's state parks were established by citizens with a can-do attitude. These were the forward thinkers who took the initiative to preserve these special spaces. The can-do attitude of a century ago has faded to a let-government-do-it mentality, but letting government do it seems to have failed. Let us embrace a will-do attitude. Iowans need to partner with government. We need to make the next hundred years of our state parks a century of pride, ensuring a heritage that brings back the spirit of America and a reverence for our land.

# Acknowledgments

The Iowa Parks Foundation extends its deepest gratitude to the following donors and contributors whose generosity made this book possible.

**FINANCIAL SUPPORTERS**
Kevin and Holly Szcodronski
Les and Ann Raisch
William C. Knapp Charitable Foundation
Easter Family Fund
G. David and Trudy Holman Hurd Fund
Patty and Jim Cownie Charitable Fund
Ohnward Bancshares, Inc./Maquoketa State Bank
Bob and Kay Riley
Iowa Natural Heritage Foundation
Ernest and Florence Sargent Family Foundation
Meredith Corporation Foundation
RDG Planning and Design
Keep Iowa Beautiful
Ramsey Subaru
Carole and Duke Reichardt
Mark and Susan Ackelson
Gerry and Pat Schnepf
Michael Carrier

**SPECIAL THANKS TO**
Sherry Arntzen, Travis Baker, Brian Button, Casey Kohrt, and Julie Tack, Iowa Department of Natural Resources
Holly Carver
Don Craig
John Doershuk, Office of the State Archaeologist
Cale Edwards, Hancock County Conservation Board
Bonnie Friend, Wayne County Conservation Board
Dan Heissel, Woodbury County Conservation Board
Phil Kerr and Richard Langel, Iowa Geological Survey
Bruce Lindner, Wright County Conservation Board
Steve Martin, Butler County Conservation Board
John Pearson
Ann Raisch
Kay Scheffler
Leland Searles
Sioux County Conservation Board
Mary Stein
Ginalie Swaim
Warren Terpstra
David Wehde, Johnson County Conservation Board
Hank Zaletel

# Navigating This Book

Perhaps the best way to navigate this book is to follow your curiosity, although we hope you also get lost in the photographs. The heart of the book features the artistry of well-known nature photographers Carl Kurtz, Brian Gibbs, Don Poggensee, and Larry Stone as well as many other accomplished photographers with a good eye and a love of Iowa's landscape. They help tell the stories of Iowa's state parks, recreation areas, preserves, and forests. And see the end of the book for historic photographs of iconic park architecture and current photographs highlighting the contributions of park friends groups.

Preceding the photo-essays, a historical overview sets the stage by explaining how Iowa's state parks began and then grew to become an expansive system. Five essays on key aspects of our park system follow the overview, written by authors whose names will be familiar to many: "Geological Foundations" by geologist Jean C. Prior, "Ecosystems of Iowa's Parks and Preserves" by ecologist and science writer Cornelia F. Mutel, "Biodiversity, Conservation, and the Land Ethic" by ecologist John Pearson, "Archaeology of Iowa's State Parks and Preserves" by archaeologist William E. Whittaker, and "The

Landscape Architectural Design of Iowa's State Parks" by landscape architect Heidi Hohmann. For those who want to dive deeper, a list of publications available in public libraries, at booksellers, or online appears at the end of the book.

Throughout the book, we refer to the administrative agency with jurisdiction over state lands and waters by the name applicable at the relevant time. From 1918 to 1935, that agency was the Iowa State Board of Conservation. In 1935, the board was merged with the Fish and Game Commission to become the Iowa Conservation Commission. The State Preserves Act of 1965 authorized a citizens board, the State Preserves Advisory Board, appointed by the governor and placed under the commission's jurisdiction. In 1986, the Iowa Department of Natural Resources superseded the Iowa Conservation Commission when the commission was merged with the Department of Water, Air and Waste Management. The authorizing legislation established two new governor-appointed advisory commissions: the Natural Resources Commission, which assumed the responsibilities of the Iowa Conservation Commission, and the Environmental Protection

Commission. Under the 1986 reorganization, the State Preserves Advisory Board also advises the Iowa Department of Natural Resources.

Finally, a note about wildlife management areas, which are mentioned in passing throughout but not featured. This does not mean that wildlife areas are less important. Quite the opposite: they protect critical wildlife habitats, provide additional recreational opportunities, and are increasingly essential to sustaining healthy parks and preserves. However, wildlife areas developed somewhat independently from the state park system. They are integral to the larger environmental history of Iowa's lands and waters, but this book commemorates the origins of our state parks and the other state lands that evolved from them.

# IOWA STATE PARKS

# A Brief History of Iowa's State Park System

REBECCA CONARD

Parks are so deeply ingrained in our contemporary landscape that we seldom question their origins; they are just there. But when we are inside public parks, we recognize their value as outdoor spaces freely available for recreation, exploration, and contemplation. It was this sense of the value of conserving public lands that compelled a group of Iowans to call for a system of state parks more than a century ago.

Every movement begins with a call to action, and for Iowa that call came from Thomas Macbride, professor of natural sciences at the University of Iowa. In 1895, speaking before the Iowa Academy of Science, Macbride articulated his vision of a statewide system of county or rural parks—public parks away from cities that could promote health and happiness, provide places to learn about the natural world, and preserve "something of the primeval nature" of Iowa. Over the course of two decades, Macbride's

vision swelled and meshed with the broader national park and forestry movement. New conservation organizations, such as the Iowa Park and Forestry Association, which became the Iowa Conservation Association, and established organizations, such as the Iowa Academy of Science and the Iowa State Horticultural Society, brought expertise to the movement. The campaign for and passage of the National Park Service Act in 1916 gave advocates confidence that the time was right for action at the state level. They drew inspiration from the work of U.S. Representative John F. Lacey of Oskaloosa, who had been instrumental in passing landmark conservation legislation at the federal level.

Macbride's voice and Lacey's example empowered a generation of leaders and organizers, including botanist Louis Pammel and forester Gilmour B. MacDonald, both of Iowa State University, who were actively involved in drafting the bill that became the

1

1917 State Park Act. The act authorized a process "to establish public parks . . . upon the shores of lakes, streams or other waters of the state, or at any other places which have by reason of their location become historic or which are of scientific interest, or by reason of their natural scenic beauty or location become adapted therefor." It also authorized the governor to appoint a State Board of Conservation with responsibility for investigating places that possessed these qualities. In 1919, the act was amended to give the board authority for establishing state parks. Another amendment in 1921 gave the board jurisdiction over "all meandered lakes and streams . . . and state lands bordering thereon."

Governor W. L. Harding made the first appointments to the Iowa State Board of Conservation in 1918, and Louis Pammel served as its vigorous and steadfast chair until 1927. In 1919, the board issued an important report—*Iowa Parks: Conservation of Iowa Historic, Scenic and Scientific Areas*—which identified nine areas that had been purchased or donated for state parks and ninety-nine areas that "responsible citizens" had proposed for acquisition. In 1920, two state parks were dedicated: Backbone State Park in Delaware County on May 28 and Lacey-Keosauqua State Park in Van Buren County on October 26 and 27. These dedications marked the beginning of Iowa's state park system.

In 1931, when the board issued its second major report, there were forty parks in the system. Of the forty, twenty-five had been listed in the 1919 report. From the beginning, the board invited park proposals from citizens groups, which greatly widened its perspective on the value of state parks. The State Park Act did not mention creating parks specifically for recreation, in part because everyone assumed that state parks would be open to the public to use. However, the uses that early park advocates had in mind were passive in nature, such as hiking, fishing, and picnicking. It quickly became clear that many Iowans wanted state parks for more active forms of recreation, such as golf, camping, and swimming, which required dedicated spaces and special facilities. Throughout the 1920s, the board focused its attention on land acquisition and, in doing so, leveraged state funds by asking communities to share the cost. This practice, along with the growing popularity of automobile tourism, increased public demand for more intensive recreational use. Modest annual appropriations limited what the board could do, so park development focused on the basics: building access roads and hiking trails, creating picnic areas with tables and fire pits, providing what were politely called comfort stations, and perhaps erecting shelter houses for group gatherings. By the end of the decade, however, a few campgrounds and golf courses were in evidence.

The 1930s are remembered for the tremendous development of national, state, and local parks. During the Great Depression, the federal government created several programs to ease economic distress by employing people to restore public lands and build public works. The programs that most benefited parks were the Civilian Conservation

Corps, which employed young men and World War I veterans; the Civil Works Administration, the Public Works Administration, and the Works Progress Administration, which created jobs for men and some women; and the National Youth Administration, a small program for teenage boys. In Iowa alone, federal programs aided the construction of at least a thousand structures in state parks, everything from architecturally distinctive stone-and-timber day-use lodges to campgrounds, artificial lakes, beach houses, and toboggan runs to culverts inconspicuously tucked under park roads and trails. Most of these structures are still in use and listed on the National Register of Historic Places, and many buildings have been restored or carefully renovated for new uses. Federal assistance also helped the state acquire more than 11,000 acres for forestry purposes, the beginning of Iowa's state forests. The legacy of these federal programs is one that park visitors continue to enjoy, not just in Iowa but at national, state, and local parks across the country.

Iowa was prepared to take immediate advantage of federal aid because the Iowa Twenty-five Year Conservation Plan was completed in 1933, the same year that federal work relief programs began. This visionary plan both reaffirmed the conservation value that had given rise to the state park system and fully embraced the recreational value of state lands and waters. It proposed a system of parks, preserves, wildlife refuges, public hunting grounds, and highway waysides that would be evenly distributed across the state and managed for conservation. "Every phase of

public recreation," the plan asserted, "is dependent upon three major correlative factors—erosion control, the conservation of surface waters, and the conservation of forest and small cover on the lands." The plan also recommended unified management by merging the responsibilities of the State Board of Conservation and the Fish and Game Commission into one state agency. In 1935, these two bodies were consolidated as the Iowa Conservation Commission.

Between 1931 and 1941, the system grew from forty to approximately ninety areas. World War II curtailed land acquisition and park development between 1942 and 1946. However, postwar prosperity triggered a boom in outdoor recreation. As a result, the number of visitors to national and state parks soared. In 1946, 1.5 million people visited Iowa state parks. The figure rose to 3.3 million in 1951 and nearly 7 million in 1960. Three dynamics influenced the evolving system in the postwar era: public demand for water-based recreation, increasing concern for protecting areas of scientific or cultural importance, and a growing realization that caring for the system was costly.

One specific recommendation of the Twenty-five Year Conservation Plan was to create artificial lakes, mainly in southern Iowa, to augment the natural lakes in northern Iowa. The state built six new artificial lake parks in the 1950s—a seventh was donated—and they proved to be exceptionally popular. Between 1940 and 1980, approximately twenty parks with artificial lakes were either added to the system or redesigned to include a lake. Three of these parks were created in partnership with the U.S. Army Corps of Engineers, which between 1957 and the late 1960s built four flood-control reservoirs on the Des Moines, Iowa, and Chariton Rivers.

Thomas Macbride's vision of county parks took on new importance in the postwar era. In the 1950s, the Iowa Conservation Commission had begun enlisting civic groups, sporting clubs, and youth organizations to help with soil and water conservation efforts, wildlife programs, outdoor recreation, and conservation education. Counties also had begun to establish public parks. These two trends ripened into proposals for a more formal state-local partnership as the state system expanded and the commission struggled to meet its management responsibilities. Various legislative proposals culminated in the 1955 County Conservation Act, which empowered counties to levy taxes for park funds and create county conservation boards with the authority to acquire and manage parks, preserves, playgrounds, recreation centers, forests, and wildlife areas. Under this law, the Iowa Conservation Commission began to transfer management of smaller state parks and other state-owned lands to county conservation boards through long-term agreements.

Also in the postwar decades, conservationist thinking meshed with growing concerns about environmental threats to lands, waters, wildlife, and human health. A new round of conservation activity in the state began: the Iowa Chapter of The Nature Conservancy was established in 1963, and in 1964 Governor Harold Hughes appointed an advisory Committee on Conservation of Outdoor Resources. Most important, in 1965 the legislature passed the State Preserves Act, which revived and amplified the conservation intent of the 1917 State Park Act. The State Preserves Act authorized a system of preserves to provide the highest form of protection to places that harbored important native plants or animals, geologic features, archaeological remains, historic sites, or exceptionally scenic areas. Because many of these places were already in the state park system, the preserves system has evolved with it.

Only three new state parks have been added since 1980, although the system as a whole has continued to expand. The critical importance of federal programs is often mentioned in relation to park build-out in the 1930s, but federal aid has been a factor in acquiring and managing state lands since then. Public lands management has also become more complex. By 1970, the Iowa Conservation Commission was working with an increasing number of county conservation boards and an increasing range of federal agencies in an era of increasing federal and state environmental regulations. Thus when Governor Terry Branstad reorganized state government top to bottom in 1986, the Iowa Conservation Commission and the Department of Water, Air and Waste Management were combined into a comprehensive Iowa Department of Natural Resources. Creating this superagency entailed establishing separate bureaus for parks and preserves, forestry, and fish and wildlife but did not diminish the need for coordination.

Water quality is perhaps the best example of

the complexity of public lands management. Public attention to Iowa's water-quality problems often focuses on natural and artificial lakes in state parks. As early as 1946, the legislature passed a law enabling the Iowa Conservation Commission to work with private landowners to improve the watersheds of state-owned lakes. Since then, water-quality issues have steadily intensified in scope and severity, and efforts to address them have grown in proportion. In 2006, the Iowa Department of Natural Resources launched the latest and largest of these efforts: the Lake Restoration and Water Quality Improvement Program. Through projects that require research, collaboration with federal and local government agencies, and cooperation from private landowners, the program aims to significantly improve the water quality of more than 130 of the publicly owned lakes in Iowa. In many respects, individual lake restoration projects have become laboratories for tackling Iowa's most critical environmental concern.

Restoration, enhancement, and partnership have become the new management key words: restoring the lands and waters that have been placed in this public trust; enhancing state parks for even greater appeal to an increasingly diverse range of visitors; and partnering with ever more government agencies, nongovernmental organizations, and private citizens groups. To meet these responsibilities, Iowa has augmented state appropriations with special-source revenue, most notably gaming receipts, a portion of which are directed to state lands and waters through the Rebuild Iowa Infrastructure Fund and

the Environment First Fund. In 2010, Iowa voters approved an amendment to the state constitution that created a permanent trust fund for Iowa's natural resources through a small increase in the sales tax. To date, the tax increase has not been implemented, and the Natural Resources and Outdoor Recreation Trust Fund so far exists in name only.

In the century since Iowa dedicated its two flagship parks, the state's conservation and recreation lands have grown to encompass nearly 385,000 acres. These open spaces draw more than 15 million annual day-use visitors who come for recreation, exploration, and contemplation. The state parks of the 1920s have evolved into a broad array of state lands and waters that are classified as parks, recreation areas, preserves, forests, and wildlife management areas. Frequently, they are located side by side, although each classification has different management guidelines that are carried out by professionally trained staff, sometimes in partnership with other public agencies and sometimes assisted by volunteers or friends groups. Together, they represent a century of stewardship by the many people who created this legacy one step at a time.

# Geological Foundations

**JEAN C. PRIOR**

Sitting on my bookshelf is a thin, dark green, hardbound volume with faded gold letters on the spine. It opens to 528 pages of small print and big ideas. The title is *Iowa Parks: Conservation of Iowa Historic, Scenic and Scientific Areas.* The year of publishing the small print was 1919. The compiler of the big ideas was the Iowa State Board of Conservation, and the authors included geologists, botanists, historians, congressmen, editors, lawyers, university presidents, homemakers, and other "responsible citizens." A mutual collaboration of science and the public interest, the little book is notable as the beginning of the centennial milestone we commemorate with the 2020 volume now in your hands.

Of interest among this assortment of authors are both the diversity of their backgrounds and the number who were geologists. These points remind us that places of natural beauty appeal to a broad range of people, that scientists and the general public share common ground, and that geology in particular provides the foundation for many of the other "ologies" that are part of Iowa's natural and cultural history. Geology is an ever-present element of Iowa's landscape, the substrate for its native plant and animal communities, the parent of its various soil types, and the source of its underground water and rock resources.

The collaboration of 1919 bore fruit. Over the past century, Iowa has established a variety of state lands for public enjoyment. In addition to the customary recreational attractions of these sites, their landscapes, waterscapes, and underpinnings tell the geological story of Iowa. Each state park, preserve, recreation area, and forest intersects with some chapter of the state's geologic past. This past may include the warm currents of ancient oceans, the icy passage of glaciers, the gritty accumulation of windblown silt, or the sculpture of flowing water.

At the root of Iowa's diverse scenes and sediments is bedrock. The rock-hard remains of sediments once deposited along ancient sea floors, coastlines, rivers, and deltas make up Iowa's bedrock foundations. Hundreds of feet of these layered sedimentary rocks, later warped and tilted by regional geologic forces, now dip downslope toward Kansas and Oklahoma, their uptilted surfaces carved and beveled by eons of erosion. What this structural framework does for visitors to Iowa's parks and preserves across the state is to reveal a remarkable sequence of environments spanning an impressive interval of earth history from Cambrian age, 500 million years ago, to Cretaceous age 74 million years ago.

Beginning in northeast Iowa and traveling south and west, visitors to state parks and preserves will encounter landscapes underlain by sedimentary rocks of increasingly younger ages. For example, at Yellow River State Forest in Allamakee County, the spectacular gorge of the Mississippi Valley is deep enough to reveal outcrops of Cambrian age sandstone composed of rounded grains of quartz, once shuffled by shallow ocean currents. Younger, lime-rich dolomites of Ordovician age (450 million years) buttress the scenic overlooks at Pikes Peak State Park in Clayton County and the Mines of Spain State Recreation Area in Dubuque County.

Farther south into Jackson County, however, the picturesque overlooks at Bellevue State Park are upheld by still younger lime-rich dolomites of Silurian age (440 million years). These rocks also show off their resistance to erosion along the high narrow ridge at Backbone State Park in Delaware County. Their inherent fractures, however, make these carbonate rocks susceptible to the slow dissolving action of groundwater, seen and felt in the cool moist recesses of Maquoketa Caves State Park in Jackson County.

Still younger and farther west are the abundant and diverse marine fossils found weathering from soft limey Devonian age (375 million years) shale at Fossil and Prairie Park State Preserve in Floyd County. To the south in Van Buren County, the great bend in the Des Moines River curves past Lacey-Keosauqua State Park, exposing limestone and sandstone of Mississippian age (330 million years). Even farther west, the sand once carried in river channels of Pennsylvanian age (310 million years) now forms the scenic bluffs of cross-bedded sandstone in Cedar Bluffs Natural Area and State Preserve in Mahaska County and Ledges State Park in Boone County. Finally, the youngest of Iowa's sedimentary rocks are seen in the thin, chalky, clam-rich limestones of Cretaceous age (100 million years) exposed along the base of the hills at Stone State Park in Woodbury County.

There is one last surprise in this pattern of visible encounters with sedimentary bedrock in Iowa: the low, wind-polished, reddish outcrops of Sioux Quartzite in the far corner of northwest Iowa at Gitchie Manitou State Preserve in Lyon County. Composed of rounded grains of quartz firmly cemented with silica, this is the oldest bedrock seen at the land surface anywhere in Iowa. These outcroppings occur along the southern flank of the Pre-Cambrian age (1.6 billion years) Sioux Ridge, an ancient bedrock feature trending east-west across parts of Minnesota and South Dakota against which Iowa's younger sedimentary rocks lie.

What's more, Iowa lies in the midst of some much

younger geological events: advancing glaciers from the Hudson Bay region of Canada. Our state straddles the outer limits of most of the major glacial advances into the Upper Midwest, between 2.6 million years ago and 14,000 years ago. Iowa's oldest glacial deposits (Pre-Illinoian age, older than 500,000 years) underlie the steeply rolling terrain across most of southern Iowa. These glacial plains of pebbly silt and clay, now well drained and deeply carved, characterize the slopes of Pammel State Park in Madison County and Nine Eagles State Park in Decatur County.

When more recent Wisconsin age glaciers (40,000 to 15,000 years) loomed just north of Iowa, silt-laden glacial outwash was being carried down the broad Missouri River during seasons of melting. Sediments strewed along the floodplain during low-flow winters were blown from the valley on dominant west winds and accumulated in unusually thick deposits of loess along its leeward length in western Iowa. Subsequent erosion carved these massive deposits into intricate patterns of steep narrow ridges with peaks and saddles along their crests, side spurs, catstep features on unstable slopes, and steep-sided gullies. The picturesque terrain at Waubonsie, Preparation Canyon, and Stone State Parks in western Iowa clearly displays the unusual landscape features associated with this chapter of Iowa's geologic history.

A period of particularly intense glacial cold that occurred between 21,000 and 16,000 years ago produced permafrost in the ground and tundra conditions across all of northern Iowa. The once-hilly terrain was leveled out, stripped by seasonal freezing and thawing that triggered the downslope movement of waterlogged sediments. Cobbles and boulders of nonnative igneous and metamorphic rocks were uncovered by the erosional scouring; these glacial erratics lie scattered across the gently rolling open terrain of Hayden Prairie State Preserve in Howard County. Wedges of frost caused even massive blocks of bedrock to slip and rotate out of position, well displayed in the tumble of rocks within Brush Creek Canyon State Preserve in Fayette County.

Even younger landscapes of fresh glacial origin exist across north-central Iowa. Signatures of southbound surges of the Des Moines Lobe ice sheet, between 15,000 and 12,000 years ago, are clearly seen in the region's low-relief terrain, abundant lakes and wetlands, and broad arcs of hummocky hills that mark moraines along stationary glacial margins. These periodic surges were followed by stagnation and slow melting of the ice. Left behind are the prominent ice-contact features seen at Freda Haffner Kettlehole State Preserve in Dickinson County and Pilot Knob State Park in Hancock County, as well as numerous ponded wetlands as at Clear Lake State Park in Cerro Gordo County and Black Hawk State Park in Sac County, marking the eastern and western margins of the Des Moines Lobe ice. Even subtle meltwater routes can be traced among the prairie potholes at Doolittle Prairie State Preserve in Story County.

As various "ice age" (Quaternary) glaciers melted from the Iowa landscape, our modern rivers took shape. Massive floods of glacial meltwater enlarged their valleys and left abundant sand and gravel deposits along their courses. During the 14,000 years since then, sand blown from the Iowa and Cedar River floodplains, for example, has been deposited on adjoining leeward margins. These upland ridges and dunes create the special habitats seen at Marietta Sand Prairie State Preserve in Marshall County, Cedar Hills Sand Prairie State Preserve in Black Hawk County, and Behrens Ponds and Woodland State Preserve in Linn County. The natural meanderings and cutoffs along our modern rivers are seen today as oxbow lakes, especially along the Missouri River at Lewis and Clark State Park in Monona County and at Browns Lake–Bigelow Park in Woodbury County.

Native Americans were drawn to these river valleys. They occupied heights along the Mississippi River bluffs, now protected as state preserves at Toolesboro Mounds in Louisa County and Malchow Mounds in Des Moines County, and sometimes they chose lower sites on alluvial terraces within the broad valley, notably at Fish Farm Mounds State Preserve in Allamakee County. Rivers became the pathways for Iowa's exploration and settlement by Euro-Americans. An 1840s limestone quarry along the Turkey River provided building materials for Fort Atkinson, now a state preserve in Winneshiek County.

Interpreting the geology of Iowa's parks and preserves helps visitors appreciate our state's sometimes subtle, sometimes scenic differences and become aware of the variety in geologic deposits from place to place. In turn, these variations in landscape contours and their underlying geology and hydrology set the stage for fascinating, sometimes fragile natural habitats and their native plant and animal communities. This knitting together of geology and ecology is especially obvious at Turin Loess Hills, Silver Lake Fen, Mossy Glen, White Pine Hollow, Bluffton Fir Stand, and Malanaphy Springs State Preserves.

Iowans' understanding of the geological heritage of their home ground is thus awakened and absorbed through visits to state parks and preserves. These lands contain scenic views to refresh the spirit, geologic concepts to stretch the imagination, and solid geologic facts on which to build a better public understanding of the resource and environmental issues that Iowans face today.

We inherited these lands and waters from our geologic past. There are no new inspiring landscapes, rich soils, absorbent wetlands, aquifers for drinking water, or sources of needed rock and minerals being formed today, and no tropical seaways, thick sheets of glacial ice, winters of turbulent winds, rivers of meltwater torrents, or root systems of vast prairies to bring them about, at least in the foreseeable future.

Iowa's state parks and preserves are limited in their geographic extent. State budgets and programs for them are shrinking. Professional staff to care for them and interpret them are being lost. There is, on the positive side, a noticeable increase in local and county public education efforts, citizen science monitoring programs, nonprofit land trusts to protect and conserve natural areas for public enjoyment, and active volunteer naturalists and friends groups to maintain them. That tradition of "responsible citizens," first apparent in the little green book of 1919, is especially important today.

Iowa's state parks and preserves showcase the harmonies, the lessons, and the natural systems that continuously operate on the surface and beneath the ground throughout our state. As interesting as their geological ages are, these rocks and sediments are not locked in the past, and their geological lessons extend well beyond their fenced borders. Though parks and preserves are protected with legal descriptions and labeled with signs, they are not places apart in time or space. They are not separate from our urban and rural lives, marked off as we are by geometric patterns of city blocks, section-line roads, and rectangles of row crops. Rather, these parks and preserves show us, in a very direct way, something of the ongoing systems of the natural world, how things really work, and what the earth's own timescale looks like. They remind us that we need to learn to live with this natural environment and its geological heritage throughout our state. We need to always consider the basic processes of how land and water work across the natural spans of earth's horizons, depths, and time. Science and society in Iowa must continue their conversations and collaborations as first put to print in 1919, reminding us that we are part of the natural world, and that our understanding and stewardship of it need to be part of our view of life.

# Ecosystems of Iowa's Parks and Preserves

**CORNELIA F. MUTEL**

I crunch through curling oak leaves, my feet negotiating a favorite path in Lake Macbride State Park. I've lived near this park for forty years, so I know its trails well. And its woodlands, and planted prairie, and the meanders of a hidden stream that is especially inviting in early spring. I've kayaked the park's lake, noting silent green herons and yellow-flowered St. John's–wort along its shores. I've biked its lakeshore trail. In this park, during a gray-skied autumn walk, I delighted in finding green dragon—an uncommon relative of jack-in-the-pulpit—flaunting crimson berries.

My sons grew up wandering this land. The youngest regularly camped here with middle-school friends, me sleeping in a nearby tent. My eldest held his wedding reception here, spreading food-laden tables under boughs of massive white oaks. So many rich memories.

I ask myself, Why has this one small piece of Iowa needled its way into my mind and heart, when I barely notice Iowa's vast agricultural lands? I'm convinced it's the diversity of life I find here, the biodiversity, and the sense that nearly every time I visit, I am delighted by something I was not expecting. A few hundred migrating swallows dipping and dancing over the water. Loons in transit resting on the lake. Clusters of somber white pelicans bobbing on the waves. Flowering trilliums in the spring, cream gentian blossoms in the fall. A mink looping its way across a path. A female wood duck leading a clutch of downy chicks to a nearby pond. A copious variety of plants and animals live here together, creating a sense that this is how the world should be, a wholesome diversity of native species occupying a wholesome diversity of native communities.

Herein lies the immeasurable worth of this

park—and by extension the worth of all Iowa's state parks and preserves: they have become irreplaceable reservoirs of the biodiversity and functionality of Iowa's original prairies and woodlands. To better understand this, consider the amazing profusion of life that Euro-American immigrants found here in the 1830s: skeins of geese passing overhead by the millions, wedges of long-billed curlews, rivers of golden plovers, flocks of passenger pigeons large enough to darken the sky for days on end. Miles of massive savanna oaks. Prairies stretching unbroken to the distant horizon, their flowers each week parading a new subset of shapes and colors.

This abundance of life was paired with a tremendous diversity of species. Hundreds of types of flowering plants grew in Iowa's tallgrass prairies, providing homes for a great variety of mammals, reptiles, birds, microorganisms, mosses, fungi, and other life-forms. This windy sun-dried landscape was maintained by regular fire and drought, natural forces that settlers quickly learned to fear. Prairies reigned supreme over 28 million acres, about four-fifths of Iowa.

Wooded lands with their own species associations covered most of the remaining fifth. Most abundant were the fire-thinned upland oak-hickory stands scattered across south-central and eastern Iowa, places where trees found the moisture required for growth. Wooded bottomlands with many tree species followed rivers throughout the state.

Both prairie and woodland plants grew in a constantly shifting mix of communities that regularly incorporated marshes, sloughs, ephemeral ponds, and other wetlands. Each supported its own association of moisture-loving species. The small water-filled depressions called potholes were abundant in the flatlands of north-central Iowa. Rich, moist prairies could be tall enough to hide a horse or herd of cattle. In contrast, western Iowa's well-drained Loess Hills produced shorter, sparser, more drought-prone prairies with species normally found farther to the west. All told, Iowa comprised an infinite variety of species and communities.

Nineteenth-century settlers likely didn't realize that another miracle of diversity lay in the prairie soils under their boots, where dense roots stretched down 5, 10, sometimes 20 feet. The roots intertwined to form thick, tough mats that housed large numbers of bacteria, nematodes, amoebas, beetles, wasps, bees, spiders, fungi, algae, insect larvae, snails, ants, and earthworms, joined by mice and moles and badgers as well as snakes, lizards, toads, and other organisms. As this life circled through generations, decomposing organic material combined with mineral particles to create a rich topsoil, Iowa's black gold, which in the early 1800s averaged 16 inches deep.

This soil became the basis of our agricultural economy, but it did so much more. Air pockets abounded among the twining root mats, and these soaked up even heavy rainfalls like a sponge, releasing moisture reluctantly. Thus water levels rose and fell slowly, and floods were rare. When water surfaced, it ran clear, the soil particles remaining tightly held within the root matrix. These natural functions of healthy prairies—soil formation, water purification, and prevention of floods and soil erosion—are called ecosystem services. Ecosystem services also include the cycling of nutrients and energy, detoxification of pollutants and pathogens, moderation of climate and weather extremes, sequestration of carbon, insect control, pollination of flowers and crops, decomposition of wastes, and much more. Ecosystem services, freely provided by nature and fed by biodiversity, hold the world together. They make the world function.

And Iowa's prairies and woodlands had functioned well for thousands of years, their diverse life-forms and communities interacting with one another in life-affirming manners. A species might wax or wane with weather extremes, but barring major environmental change, it was ensured survival. The land itself remained robust and healthy, a model of stability and sustainability.

Iowa's Euro-American settlers were not inclined to dwell on this land's richness. Hungry for food and homes, they raised their axes and transformed woodlands into homesteads, fences, and fuel. Applying John Deere's steel moldboard plows, they sliced through prairie sods and dropped corn kernels into rough furrows. Wildlife, removed with shotguns and traps, was replaced by cattle, hogs, and other livestock.

Then came a river of ever more sophisticated mechanical implements: planters, cultivators, reapers, threshers, and more. Dredges and drainage tiles dried wetlands. By 1900, most of Iowa was being farmed. Fifty years later, tractors had replaced work horses, and synthetic pesticides, herbicides, and fertilizers were being spread on fields. Since then, the push toward greater agricultural mechanization and larger fields has erased native plant communities from most of Iowa's landscape. Only 0.1 percent of Iowa's native prairies remains today. Our original complex grasslands and interspersed woodlands, with their thousands of species and varied communities, have been largely replaced by two crops. Corn and soybeans now blanket two-thirds of Iowa.

Along with the prairie and its biodiversity went the resilient, self-sustaining landscape it once fostered. Today, Iowa's largest environmental problems—soil erosion, degrading water and air quality, and flooding—are the results of Iowa's agricultural transformation and the resulting loss of ecosystem services.

Yet although the extent and abundance of native species have shriveled, remnants of our ancient prairies and woodlands remain. Many of the best are protected on our state lands, which provide a taste of the infinite variety and inborn functions of Iowa's presettlement landscape.

Let's consider a few examples. Like most healthy prairie remnants, the 240-acre Hayden Prairie State Preserve—Iowa's largest prairie outside the Loess Hills—hosts more than 200 plant species in addition to dozens of species of grassland birds, butterflies, and other animals. This prairie includes mesic—moderately moist—and wet plant communities. In contrast, Kalsow and Doolittle Prairies are characterized by their prairie potholes; Manikowski and Marietta Sand Prairies display dry soils and communities; and Freda Haffner Kettlehole, with nearly 250 native vascular plant species, illustrates a continuum from aquatic plants in the kettlehole pond through mesic prairies on slopes to dry prairies on gravelly ridgelines.

Western Iowa's steep, well-drained Loess Hills have retained more nature than most of Iowa; the hills now boast the state's largest remaining prairies. Here expansive dry grasslands incorporate rare plants and animals typical of the droughty Great Plains. Five Ridge Prairie, Sylvan Runkel, Turin Loess Hills, Mount Talbot, and Vincent Bluff State Preserves demonstrate the typical distribution of Loess Hills prairies today: they drape over the driest sites, over ridgetops and south- and west-facing hillsides. Oak and other woodlands have overtaken moister slopes and bottomlands. Native Loess Hills prairies and woodlands are also found in Stone, Preparation Canyon, and Waubonsie State Parks and the Loess Hills State Forest.

Oak woodlands have fared better than prairies in Iowa; however, lacking the regular burning they require, few closely resemble Iowa's earlier open savannas. Yet mature oak forests, now mixed with other trees, remain at Fallen Rock, Palisades-Dows, and many more state preserves. Such woodlands and clusters of mature oaks are also common in state parks, especially older parks such as Geode, Backbone, Dolliver Memorial, and Ledges. Oak woodlands often intermingle with other types of communities such as bottomland forests, wetlands, and prairie remnants or, in parks, prairie plantings, and these additional communities enhance a site's diversity. The 63-acre

Woodman Hollow State Preserve, a forested ravine with small prairie openings, contains an amazing 500-plus plant species. Behrens Ponds and Woodland State Preserve, with its sandy soils, oaks, thickets, prairie openings, marshes, and ponds, holds more than 300 plant species in just 29 acres. Pilot Knob State Preserve, with its dry and mesic forests, also houses a boggy lake, marshes, and over 420 plant species. The beauty of most native woodlands is augmented in spring by rich wildflower displays and the singing of dozens of nesting songbirds.

The northeastern corner of Iowa, where rugged terrain excludes intensive agriculture, remains a haven for wooded state preserves: Merritt Forest, Bixby, Mossy Glen, Malanaphy Springs, and others. Echo Valley, Backbone, and Pikes Peak State Parks and the Yellow River State Forest complement the array of state lands. Here, too, on north-facing slopes sheltered from sun and heat, remnant plant communities survive from earlier glacial times. Bluffton Fir Stand State Preserve protects one of the largest remaining clusters of balsam fir in Iowa; in modern times, these trees naturally grow much farther north. The same is true of pine groves in White Pine Hollow State Preserve, which shelters more than 500 species of plants and about 90 species of summertime birds in its forests, steep-walled valleys, bluff communities, and chilly, moist slopes.

These state parks, preserves, and forests, although protected, are not free from peril. As islands floating in an agricultural sea, their streams may be polluted with silt, concentrated animal wastes, and synthetic fertilizers. Airborne pesticides and herbicides drift through their treetops. Invasive plants and animals creep in over property lines.

Yet despite these stresses, Iowa's natural lands continue to filter and store water, moderate flooding, produce pollinators, shelter nesting birds and burrowing animals, and perform other beneficial services. They carry Iowa's biodiversity into the future by providing habitat for plants, mammals, insects, and other life-forms. They stockpile Iowa's genetic materials for possible future use. Many also serve as educational and research sites. Cayler Prairie State Preserve, for example, is regularly used by Iowa Lakeside Laboratory students, as is Ames High Prairie State Preserve by high school biology classes. And because parks and preserves beg for the removal of invasives, thinning of woody growth, prescribed burning, collection of native seed, and other forms of land management, they offer humans multiple venues for positively engaging with the land and redressing prior environmental abuses.

Our parks and preserves serve as living museums and windows into the past, informing us of what Iowa once was and how it worked. And they point us toward the future, feeding visions and providing models for how we might clean our waters and deepen our topsoils, or how native species and agriculture might work together to rebuild the land's resilience and sustainability. They invite us to ask where we Iowans are going, and then they show us how we might get there.

Our parks and preserves provide respite from daily stresses, places where we can reconnect with nature's diverse residents, rhythms, and tempos. Unconvinced? Try searching for spring wildflowers in one of our woodland parks, watch the parade of summertime blossoms in a prairie preserve, or listen for nesting birds in either. Search autumn skies for raptors migrating along the Loess Hills or huge flocks of waterfowl following the Mississippi River flyway. If you are like me, you will feel yourself becoming engaged, delighted, and restored, for such activities connect us with the mysteries of nature that surround us. They are ways of coming home to Iowa. They invite tomorrow's children to discover and bond with the land, as my sons once did in our nearby park. They invite us to see the natural world in its wholeness and beauty and the planet functioning as it should be—and once again could be, if we will give it a chance.

# Biodiversity, Conservation, and the Land Ethic

**JOHN PEARSON**

Fog drifts slowly through the glade of ancient cedars as I pick my way along the narrow ridge of the Backbone, stepping carefully across rugged blocks of lichen-splashed limestone. Arriving at the edge of an escarpment, I gaze across the forested valley of the Maquoketa River and feel a tingle of vertigo, the thrill of exploration, and a humbling sense of awe. Although I am alone, I am standing with the spirits of early naturalists Thomas Macbride, Bohumil Shimek, and Louis Pammel, who likely stood in this very spot a hundred years ago and were inspired by the same splendid landscape—inspired enough to devote years of their lives to establishing this place as the first state park in Iowa's history, Backbone State Park. The system of parks and preserves initiated with Backbone now protects many more inspirational landscapes supporting a rich flora and fauna that comprise an important part of Iowa's biological diversity. Let's look more closely at this legacy.

Biodiversity is the variety of life on earth or on a significant region of it . . . like Iowa! How many species inhabit our state? Many of us are familiar with common plants and animals like oak trees, deer, cardinals, monarch butterflies, morel mushrooms, and garter snakes, but the full number of species in Iowa is surprising to most people: more than 1,800 vascular plants (including 94 trees, 114 shrubs, 377 grasses and sedges, 51 ferns, and over 1,000 wildflowers), 271 mosses, more than 7,000 fungi (including nearly 500 lichens), 397 birds, 149 fish, 71 mammals, 67 reptiles and amphibians, 125 butterflies, approximately 2,100 moths, over 300 bees, 55 mosquitoes, 46 mussels, 180 snails, and many untallied thousands of species of other invertebrates and microorganisms. Some of the common species—like deer, crows, and poison ivy—are well adapted to the modern Iowa landscape of cities, towns, farms, and roads, but others—like lady's slipper orchids and prairie skippers—require special natural habitats in which to survive.

Iowa's state parks and other conservation lands—preserves, state forests, and wildlife areas—play an important role in preserving the state's biodiversity by providing natural habitats for thousands of native species, including many that are rare and vulnerable. In fact, this was one of the founding principles of the state park system. As early as 1895, Thomas Macbride—professor of natural history at the University of Iowa, president of the Iowa Academy of Science, and a founder of Iowa Lakeside Laboratory later commemorated as the father of conservation in Iowa—envisioned a threefold mission for parks: "to promote health and happiness, to educate, and most important, to preserve something of the primeval nature of Iowa." Louis Pammel—professor of botany at Iowa State University and also president of the Iowa Academy of Science—became the first chair of the Iowa State Board of Conservation, which was established by the 1917 State Park Act "to investigate places in Iowa, valuable as objects of natural history." Pammel noted that "the persons who framed the law had in mind the preservation of animals, rare plants, unique trees, some unique geological formations, the preservation of Indian mounds, rare old buildings where Iowa history was made . . . to show generations yet unborn what Iowa had in the way of prairie, valley, lake, and river."

Have state parks and other conservation lands achieved their goal of preserving Iowa's biodiversity? One way of assessing biodiversity is to inventory and count the species present in protected areas, a challenging task tackled by numerous botanists and zoologists over the past century. Although vascular plants are only one of many groups of species that collectively comprise biodiversity, they are typically the easiest to observe and have been comprehensively tallied in many parks and preserves across Iowa. Their numbers are impressive. Among prairie preserves, botanists have found 219 native species in Cayler Prairie, 220 in Hayden Prairie, 222 in Steele Prairie, 225 in Doolittle Prairie, and 278 in Williams Prairie. Due in part to their larger sizes and greater topographic relief, which provide more microhabitats, forested parks and preserves boast even higher numbers: 364 native species in Pilot Knob State Park, 399 in Bixby State Preserve, 508 in White Pine Hollow State Preserve, 562 in Backbone State Park, and 599 in Ledges State Park. Surveys for other organisms have been spotty, but highlights of past findings include 17 species of reptiles and amphibians in Behrens Ponds and Woodland State Preserve, 42 butterflies in Stone State Park, 87 bees in Anderson Prairie State Preserve, over 100 mosses and liverworts in Bixby State Preserve, 117 lichens in White Pine Hollow State Preserve, and 406 fungi in Pilot Knob State Park.

These counts of local diversity include many species that are common across the state as well as some that are extremely rare. Rare species are more vulnerable to loss than common ones, so another way to assess the contribution of conservation lands to the preservation of biodiversity is to examine how many of Iowa's rarest species are contained in these holdings. Of the 386 plant species officially listed by the state of Iowa as endangered, threatened, or of special concern, 120 (31 percent) have been observed in state parks, including 2 classified as federally threatened (rare in the nation, not just in Iowa): northern wild monkshood and prairie bush clover. Of the 118 animal species on the list, 39 (33 percent) have been observed there, including the federally endangered Iowa Pleistocene snail. When all conservation lands are considered, including preserves, forests, and wildlife areas of state, federal, and county ownership, the numbers jump to 312 plant species (81 percent) and 111 animal species (94 percent), including 2 more federally threatened plants: the eastern and western prairie fringed orchids.

State parks have indeed contributed to the preservation of rare plant and animal species in Iowa, and their contribution has been greatly augmented by other conservation lands. State parks figure very largely in the protection of particular species. One of the most notable examples is creeping sedge, a rare wetland plant whose only population in the state is in Pilot Knob State Park. Another noteworthy example is the blue-spotted salamander: of only two known populations in the state, one occurs in George Wyth Memorial State Park. Many state parks are heavily forested, providing prime habitat for the northern long-eared bat, a federally endangered species that prefers deep woods more than any of the other eight bat species in the state.

However, because not all species observed in the

past are still present today, these numbers do not reveal the whole story. The southern red-backed vole formerly occurred in Pilot Knob State Park but has not been seen there since the 1980s, possibly due to the maturation of early successional woodland into old forest. Federally threatened piping plovers once nested on a sandspit in Lake Manawa State Park but were last observed there in 1945, before the Missouri River was dammed upstream and its channel narrowed for navigation; without fluctuating flows spreading across a wide floodplain, creation of new sandbars was curtailed while former sandbars were overtaken with dense vegetation unsuitable for plovers. Populations of small butterflies known as prairie skippers have sharply declined on Loess Hills prairies, including those in Stone State Park and Waubonsie State Park. Two skipper species now listed as federally endangered have completely vanished from Iowa: the Dakota skipper was last observed at Cayler Prairie State Preserve in 1992, the Poweshiek skipperling at Hoffman Prairie State Preserve in 2007. Some conservationists speculate that excessive use of prescribed burns and the drift of pesticides from farm fields have been detrimental to these skippers, but the exact cause of their decline and disappearance— an effect observed universally across different management regimes and simultaneously across numerous midwestern states—remains unknown.

If parks and other conservation lands are valuable yet imperfect refuges, is there a way to improve their ability to maintain biodiversity? Yes, there is. Conservation biology shows that large contiguous blocks of habitat retain species more effectively than small isolated tracts, so one solution for the long-term preservation of biodiversity is to seek opportunities for enlarging the size of land areas managed as natural habitats. Examples of formerly isolated parks and preserves that have benefited from the subsequent establishment of additional public conservation lands include White Pine Hollow State Preserve, Cayler Prairie State Preserve, Lacey-Keosauqua State Park, and Preparation Canyon State Park.

White Pine Hollow State Preserve (792 acres) is now adjoined by the White Pine Hollow Wildlife Management Area (188 acres) and only a quarter mile from Ram Hollow Wildlife Management Area (819 acres), forming a 1,799-acre complex of rugged forested valleys in northeast Iowa.

Cayler Prairie State Preserve's original 160 acres are now connected to the Cayler Prairie Wildlife Management Area (971 acres) and Santee Prairie Wildlife Management Area (456 acres) within two miles of Yager Slough Waterfowl Production Area (503 acres), Dugout Creek Wildlife Management Area (1,126 acres), and the West Okoboji Wetland Complex (346 acres); together, they form a 3,562-acre complex of native prairie, grassland, fens, and marshes flanking the Little Sioux River in northwest Iowa.

The 1,653 acres of Lacey-Keosauqua State Park are connected to the Keosauqua Unit of Shimek State Forest (921 acres), Lake Sugema Wildlife Management Area (3,915 acres), and Lake Sugema County Park (1,446 acres), making up a 7,935-acre complex of forest, grassland, riverfront, and lake in southeast Iowa.

Preparation Canyon State Park (344 acres), once a small isolated tract, is now an integral part of the Loess Hills State Forest (11,692 acres); the two comprise a 12,036-acre complex of native prairie, oak woodland, and valley bottomland in the Loess Hills of western Iowa.

These examples feature publicly owned conservation lands, but private lands have a major role to play in the long-term preservation of Iowa's biodiversity. Indeed, it will be impossible to maintain 100 percent of Iowa's species on only the 2.5 percent of its land that is public. The cooperation of private landowners in managing the overall landscape for conservation of biodiversity is and will continue to be an important boon for nature in Iowa. In particular, the preservation of biodiversity would be greatly enhanced wherever management of public conservation lands could be coupled with environmental stewardship of their private surroundings. The Waterman Prairie Complex in northwest Iowa is an outstanding example of a large public-private landscape benefiting from the partnership of public and private land managers to preserve and restore its extensive natural prairies and woodlands.

So why does preserving biodiversity matter? There are several answers. The most human-focused one is that wild species hold genetic resources that may become useful to us in the future for invigorating crops and providing natural sources of new medicines, perhaps even a cure for cancer. Crucially, these advances may exist in species not yet utilized or even discovered. Keeping open the option of discovering their future values by preserving biodiversity in general is in our own best interest. As conservationist Aldo Leopold noted in his Round River essay, "To keep every cog and wheel is the first precaution of intelligent tinkering."

A more compelling answer is the moral argument that Leopold advanced in *Sand County Almanac* as the land ethic. Just as we as citizens of a human society have determined that we should not harm each other, we can also choose to apply our ethical behavior to the nonhuman world. As Leopold writes: "All ethics so far evolved rest upon a single premise: that the individual is a member of a community of interdependent parts. The land ethic simply enlarges the boundaries of the community to include soils, waters, plants, and animals, or collectively: the land. . . . A land ethic, then, reflects the existence of an ecological conscience, and this in turn reflects a conviction of individual responsibility for the health of the land. Health is the capacity of the land for self-renewal. Conservation is our effort to understand and preserve this capacity."

Citizens of Iowa have acted to establish a system of conservation lands that protects biodiversity in the form of parks, preserves, forest reserves, and wildlife areas. State parks in particular serve as a gateway for people to enter the natural world, explore its beauty, experience its diversity, and become aware of the value of lands devoted largely to the conservation of nature. This hundredth anniversary of Iowa's state parks serves as a grand opportunity to appreciate what previous generations have provided for us and what we can provide for future generations.

# Archaeology of Iowa's State Parks and Preserves

WILLIAM E. WHITTAKER

Some of Iowa's most significant archaeological sites are within our state parks and preserves; this is not an accident. In the 1920s and 1930s, Charles Keyes, the founding father of Iowa archaeology, lobbied the Iowa State Board of Conservation and the Iowa Conservation Commission to find archaeological sites on state land and to purchase land for the preservation of these sites; many of these purchases became state parks.

State park and preserve lands have a number of inherent advantages when it comes to archaeology. Because they are owned by the state, they are protected by guidelines for the identification, protection, and investigation of archaeological sites. Most other land in Iowa has no such protection. Private landowners have no obligation to preserve or protect sites they own unless human remains are present. Only about 2.5 percent of the state of Iowa

has been archaeologically surveyed in some way, but 26 percent of state park and preserve lands have been. Iowa as a whole has 30,000 recorded sites, about one for every 1,190 acres. Astonishingly, recorded archaeological sites are 17 times as common in state parks and preserves—685 recorded archaeological sites occur in state parks and preserves, about one site for every 70 acres.

State parks and preserves typically include areas with scenic beauty, river valleys, and uncommon landforms, a diverse array of ecosystems that were attractive to both Native Americans and early settlers. The basic criteria for selecting land for a state park also select for the criteria that prehistoric peoples used in choosing locations for their camps and villages. Substantial prehistoric Native American sites are almost always located near a variety of resources. An ideal setting for a large prehistoric village would be the high terrace of a wide river near expanses of wetlands, forests, and upland prairies—places where prehistoric peoples could easily grow crops, catch fish, harvest wetland plants and animals, and hunt deer, bison, and other game, all within easy walking distance of their village.

Humans have thrived in Iowa for at least 13,000 years. They arrived as the glaciers were receding and over millennia transformed themselves from highly mobile hunters and gatherers into farmers living in large villages. Occasionally we are lucky enough to find traces of the sites they left behind. Parks and preserves often contain sites with excellent preservation, where features such as prehistoric houses, burials, and hearths remain buried and intact. In order for an archaeological site to be preserved, it needs to be buried quickly before bone, charcoal, seeds, and other organic material decay, and this material has to remain safely buried until careful archaeological excavation exposes it.

Most of Iowa has terrible archaeological site preservation, consisting of upland farm fields where the soil was stable prehistorically but highly erosional in the modern era, which means that human living surfaces generally weren't buried quickly and have likely been affected by plowing and erosion. Not surprisingly, most parks and preserves were not established in upland plowed fields; rather, they are centered on undeveloped or underdeveloped natural areas with terraces, stream bottoms, and remote landforms, all locations where prehistoric sites were more likely to be buried quickly and then not disturbed by the plow or development in more recent times.

Some of the largest and most informative archaeological research projects include state park and preserve lands. Archaeological surveys at Honey Creek State Park at Rathbun Lake and Elk Rock State Park at Lake Red Rock have been ongoing since the U.S. Army Corps of Engineers began some of the earliest systematic surveys of Iowa in 1949. Since then, colleges and universities have led larger survey efforts, including Iowa State University's survey of Ledges and Big Creek State Parks in the early 1970s, Luther College's survey of Pikes Peak State Park in the late 1970s, Illinois State University's survey of Pilot Knob State Park in 1991, and, more recently, the University of Iowa Office of the State Archaeologist's survey of Lake Darling State Park from 2009 to 2011. The OSA helped establish the Glenwood Archaeological State Preserve through survey and research from 2008 to 2012; this preserve includes dozens of semisubterranean earth lodges dating to AD 1100 to 1300 and may be ancestral to historically known Great Plains tribes such as the Arikara and Pawnee.

Major excavations include those at the Lake Darling site, where archaeologists identified three occupation horizons, the youngest an Early to Middle Woodland period (800 BC–AD 400) occupation that contained pottery, points, heated rock, a storage pit, and other evidence of intensive village life. Below this was a Middle Archaic occupation, dating to about 7,500 to 5,000 years ago. Chert was used for stone tools, and chert sourcing indicates that the residents were more mobile and the site was less intensively occupied and more ephemeral than we would expect for preagricultural hunters and gatherers. The oldest horizon, below the Middle Archaic, could be Early Archaic or Paleoindian. We don't know for sure because there were no time-diagnostic artifacts or charcoal to radiocarbon-date, but it was more than 7,500 years old. This level contained so few artifacts that it was impossible to determine what the occupants were doing at the site. A display case at the Lake Darling Conservation District's office shows some of the findings and artifacts.

The rock shelters and caverns at Maquoketa Caves State Park provided some of the earliest evidence of the length of time the human occupation of Iowa has spanned. In the nineteenth century, amateur archaeologists were amazed at the depth of finds, and from these sites Iowa's earliest artifact seriation sequence emerged, tracing the changes in stone tools and ceramics over thousands of years. The data collected by Paul Sagers, an amateur archaeologist who made careful excavations of several Maquoketa rock shelters, revealed how artifacts recovered from deeper—and therefore older—levels changed stylistically from thick-walled Woodland pottery with simple decoration to shallower—and therefore younger—levels containing thinner and more elaborately decorated Oneota pottery.

Burial mounds are the most noticeable prehistoric features on the landscape. Mounds are usually conical in shape, but they can also be linear or animal-shaped effigies. Many state parks contain significant groups of Native American burial mounds, including Pikes Peak and Dolliver Memorial State Parks. Some state preserves, such as Fish Farm Mounds, Malchow Mounds, Gitchie Manitou, Turkey River Mounds, and Toolesboro Mounds, were created specifically to protect burial mounds. These mounds are grave markers and should be treated with the same respect as any cemetery.

Before Iowa enacted the Iowa Burials Protection Act of 1976, the first law in the world protecting Native American graves, mounds were often excavated. Extensive excavations at Turkey River in the 1960s identified extreme variation in mortuary practices, with several mutilated skeletons and evidence of ritual treatment of the dead. When road grading in 1972 for Honey Creek State Park ripped through numerous mounds—the bulldozer operators did not know about them until human remains were exposed—emergency excavations recovered what they could of the damaged graves, but by then the mounds were essentially destroyed. This incident led to better cooperation between the state park system and the Office of the State Archaeologist; state parks are now surveyed for archaeological sites before any ground moving occurs.

Parks and preserves also protect other types of significant archaeological sites, some on private property with no public access, which helps protect them. Hartley Fort State Preserve contains a large fortified Oneota village that was excavated several times between the 1960s and the 1990s. Wittrock Indian Village State Preserve, also on private property, contains a large thousand-year-old village within earthen embankment walls. Excavations at Wittrock by the University of Iowa and the University of Wisconsin helped define the Mill Creek culture of northwest Iowa. Mill Creek sites generally date AD 1100 to 1300 and are characterized by large villages of semisubterranean houses surrounded by defensive ditches and walls, a site layout completely unlike anything seen earlier. Mill Creek site residents were probable ancestors of later Plains tribes such as the Hidatsa and Mandan, who continued this site layout into the historic period—Lewis and Clark visited villages on the Upper Missouri River not unlike the village site occupied 500 years earlier at Wittrock.

The Mines of Spain State Recreation Area and adjacent Catfish Creek State Preserve encompass many of the mines dug by Meskwaki peoples in the 1700s and early 1800s and the graves of their leaders as well as Julien Dubuque, their French Canadian trading representative. One of the earliest scientific excavations in Iowa was the excavation of Dubuque from his grave in 1897 in order to rebury him in a new memorial. Extensive surveys by the OSA later identified more than two hundred archaeological sites in the area. Representing a later period, the Fort Atkinson State Preserve contains the well-preserved remains of the 1840 U.S. Army fort built to control and protect the Ho-Chunk (Winnebago); extensive excavations by the OSA from the 1960s through the 2000s helped identify the original fort layout and provide stunning views of the archaeological site.

In addition to archaeological sites, Iowa's state parks and preserves contain more than seventy-five sites listed in the Historic Indian Location Database, places where Native Americans were known to have lived or visited in the period since Europeans and Americans began appearing in the state. These range from the lead mines of Catfish Creek State Preserve to sites related to the 1857 Spirit Lake conflict at Gull Point State Park. There are about twenty-five camps and villages known to have been occupied by Native Americans from the 1700s to the late 1800s in state parks and preserves, including many suspected graves.

State parks and preserves not only protect Iowa's natural resources and scenic wild areas, they also protect the locations and landscapes associated with some of Iowa's most significant archaeological and historical sites. I've had the privilege of working on many of these sites, including excavating at Fort Atkinson, mapping the Malchow Mounds, and trying to find earth lodges at Glenwood, and I can attest to the enormous role that parks and preserves have in protecting our state's heritage.

# The Landscape Architectural Design of Iowa's State Parks

**HEIDI HOHMANN**

After legislation establishing Iowa's state parks was passed in 1917, conservationists like Louis Pammel found themselves confronted with a new challenge: the task of constructing the parks. Creating parks where people could experience nature—and not preserves where they would be excluded from it—meant balancing conservation with human enjoyment, a goal that Pammel rightly recognized as problematic when he asked, "How can we best treat the park so as to avoid the unnecessary tramping of thousands of visitors? How can the trails be constructed so that this wild life will be conserved?"

To address this dilemma, in 1923 the Iowa State Board of Conservation enlisted the services of landscape architects, thus beginning a long history of design in Iowa's state parks. In designing the parks, landscape architects sought to mitigate human impacts on sensitive landscapes through the artistic development of carefully targeted recreational facilities. While such an approach might seem old-fashioned in the context of today's rigorous scientific conservation efforts, their resulting designs still influence the ways we view, use, and appreciate the natural landscapes of our state parks.

Louis Pammel and the Board of Conservation turned to landscape architects to design Iowa's parks for two major reasons. One was the profession's prominent role in the park movement, which had begun in the 1850s with the design of Central Park by landscape architect Frederick Law Olmsted. Over the next half century, the movement spawned regional and metropolitan park systems, national parks, and finally state parks. Both the national and state park movements, though sometimes seen primarily as conservation efforts, were affiliated with the park movement, which usually prioritized the social and

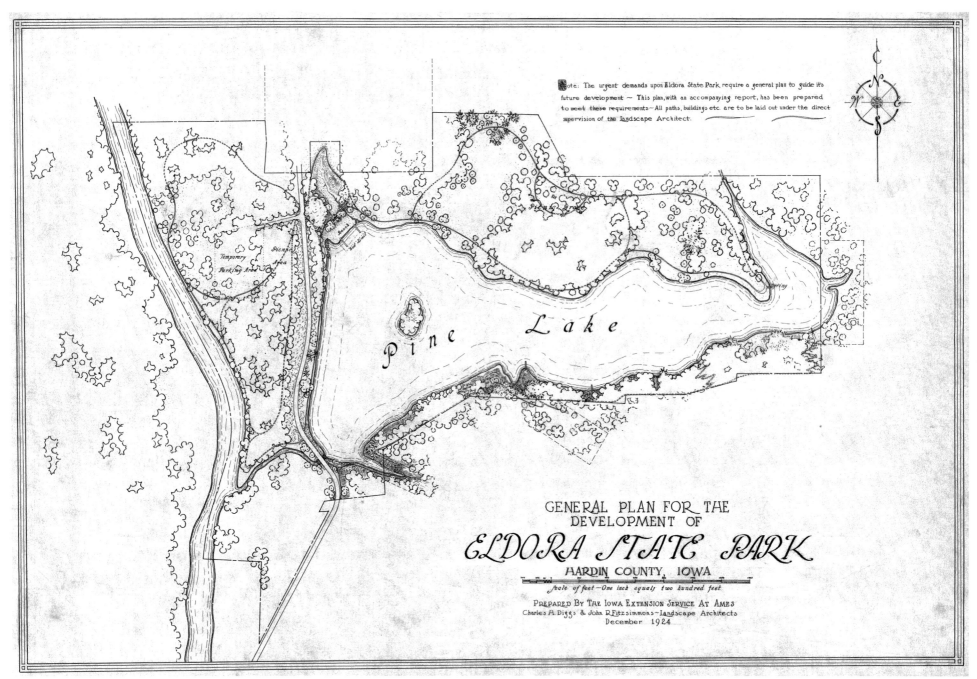

Note: The urgent demands upon Eldora State Park require a general plan to guide its future development ~ This plan, with an accompanying report, has been prepared to meet these requirements ~ All paths, buildings etc. are to be laid out under the direct supervision of the Landscape Architect.

Pine Lake

GENERAL PLAN FOR THE
DEVELOPMENT OF

ELDORA STATE PARK

HARDIN COUNTY, IOWA

Scale of feet ~ One inch equals two hundred feet

PREPARED BY THE IOWA EXTENSION SERVICE AT AMES
Charles A. Diggs & John R. Fitzsimmons ~ Landscape Architects
December 1924

aesthetic benefits of parks over their ecological benefits. In Iowa, where the conservation movement had begun in 1901 with the founding of the Iowa Park and Forestry Association, involving professional park designers—landscape architects—in state park design was a logical strategy.

A second reason was the quality and renown of Iowa's landscape architects. A landscape design program—initially called landscape gardening—had existed at Iowa State University since 1896, when it was established in the Horticulture Department. Renamed landscape architecture in 1914, the program became its own department in 1926 and quickly developed a reputation for producing "park men," trained not only in civil engineering and planting design but also in art and aesthetics. The latter abilities were particularly important to conservationists who viewed state parks as a special undertaking. Pammel, in particular, believed that "no development as ordinarily understood" should occur in a state park and that state park design required "a landscape artist in the true sense of the word." Iowa State's landscape architects fit the bill. In 1923, a legislative agreement was worked out whereby the department would consult with the state and provide plans and designs at no cost other than expenses.

Between 1920 and 1926, as the state's first thirty-eight parks were established, many department faculty, among them Charles Diggs, H. F. Kenney, and E. A. Piester, worked on state park concerns. Perhaps the most influential landscape architect, however, was John R. Fitzsimmons, who worked for more than twenty years on Iowa's state parks beginning in 1924. In his early writings on the topic, Fitzsimmons revealed typical professional predilections, viewing state parks as an extension of the urban park idea. He defined a state park in a 1926 report to the Board of Conservation as "a combination of city park and national park ideas" and in a 1925 magazine article for a professional audience as "a sanctuary wherein man can retire from his work-a-day influence and urban habits to contemplate the beauties of natural scenery." These comments reflected contemporary professional beliefs that the goal of state parks, like city parks, was to provide visitors access to nature and its uplifting scenery. In this context, recreation quite literally meant the re-creation of the human spirit rather than the active pursuits we associate with parks today. Such impressions led Fitzsimmons to develop a philosophy recommending "minimum changes in the natural features of the area . . . necessary to provide for the greater controlled use" while "emphasizing the existing elements of scenic beauty."

To accomplish these goals, Fitzsimmons and his colleagues proposed that development occur in the context of the Comprehensive Landscape Plan, which mapped out an overall vision for each park prior to any construction. Planning began with a site visit, a topographic survey, and a native plant inventory. Based on this documentation, the designers then demarked a series of key landscape units or areas of scientific or scenic interest. Each unit was identified either for use—perhaps as a site for a picnic grove, bench, trail, or campground—or for protection—

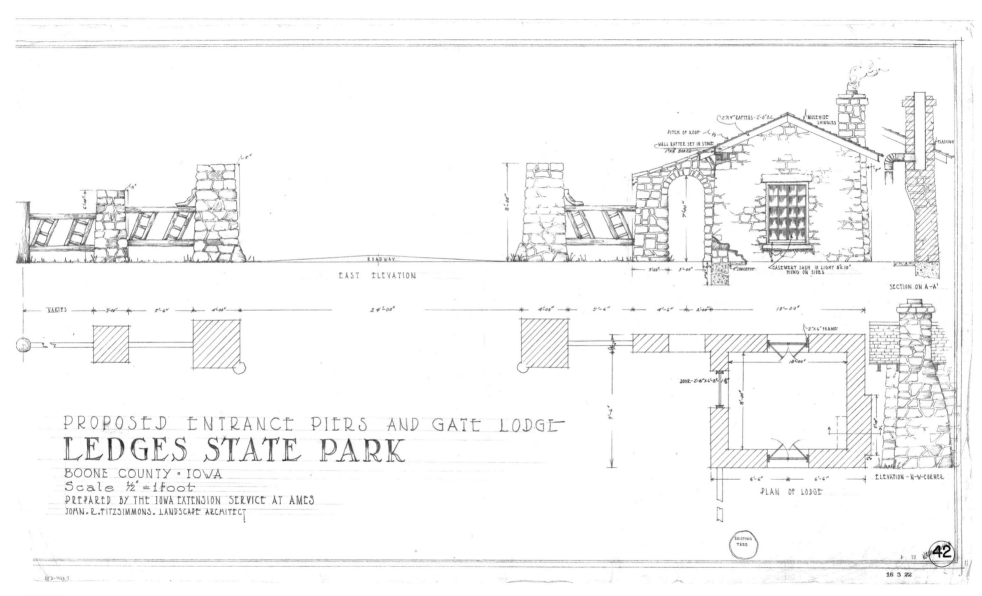

EAST ELEVATION

SECTION ON A-A'

PROPOSED ENTRANCE PIERS AND GATE LODGE
# LEDGES STATE PARK
BOONE COUNTY • IOWA
Scale ½"=1 foot
PREPARED BY THE IOWA EXTENSION SERVICE AT AMES
JOHN R. FITZSIMMONS, LANDSCAPE ARCHITECT

PLAN OF LODGE

ELEVATION-N-W-CORNER

42

perhaps via vegetation restoration or erosion prevention. Individual areas were then "brought into a whole and tied together in a systematic unit" with the design of roads and trails that linked them together.

Using a circulation system to create a holistic composition was not a new idea. It was, in fact, based on eighteenth- and nineteenth-century principles of park design, which typically prescribed a circuit drive as a means to link separate picturesque scenes into a larger, cohesive visual experience. But as automobile use increased following World War I, state park designers also realized the potential for roads to damage sensitive landscapes. In describing his design for the roads for Ledges State Park in 1924, Fitzsimmons noted that they provided "easy grades and pleasing outlooks" but caused "a concentration of human traffic and use within close range of the road." Thus road design also required mitigating the effects of access; at Ledges, the problem was counteracted by dispersing parking, camping, and picnicking areas along the length of the road.

The landscape architects also considered the aesthetic qualities of the circulation system, proposing that roads be graded along contours, not against them, and requiring engineering features to be unobtrusive or, better yet, beautiful. These objectives resulted in entry roads that wound sinuously around rock outcroppings, arched masonry bridges that crossed over streams, and stone retaining walls constructed with pockets to support native plants. As a result, the roads themselves became scenic features, sometimes on a par with the natural landscapes they traversed.

Pedestrian circulation was designed with similar care to access unique features and impressive views. At Ledges, as at other parks, Fitzsimmons planned trails as a hierarchy of primary and secondary routes to "guide and direct park visitors on side excursions and explorations in the more remote and little used parts of the park." Together, roads and trails served a dual purpose of unifying a park through the orchestration of a scenic narrative, while strategically reducing access to sensitive locations and concentrating activity in areas designed specifically for intensive use.

Intensive-use areas usually featured parking lots and facilities for park staff and visitors, including caretakers' houses, restrooms, and picnic shelters. Care was taken to ensure that these structures harmonized with their landscape context. For example, slopes around buildings and parking lots were carefully graded to blend into the surrounding terrain. Structures were designed using locally quarried stone, native timbers, vernacular building styles, and pioneer construction techniques—strategies that connected them to the landscape's settlement history. In Backbone State Park, for instance, Fitzsimmons' designs for a caretaker's house and adjacent barn adapted stylistic elements of historic agricultural buildings. A panoply of matching landscape furnishings—curbs, bollards, gateways, and signs—also accompanied every composition of larger structures, further unifying the designs.

Planting designs served a similar function. Buildings were merged with the landscape via foundation plantings of native species: Virginia creeper (woodbine) twined up pergolas and dogwoods, viburnums, and redbuds adorned building corners. Parking lots were canopied with over- and understory trees to blend in with neighboring forests. Construction scars along park roads were extensively planted in keeping with the local biome. At Pilot Knob State Park, for example, Fitzsimmons' plan for the entry road featured "mass plantings of shrubs and vines, hard maple, white oak, walnut, wild roses, sumac, prickly ash, dogwood, snowberry, bittersweet and woodbine." And wherever possible, "natural plantings of existing species" were used to restore landscapes—prairies, forests, and even bogs—replacing vegetation destroyed by "the ruthless hand of man."

Sometimes beautifully rendered large-scale drawings, these early comprehensive plans were aspirational, meant to be updated and expanded in detail as development funds became available. Although some designs were realized in the 1920s, funds in the early years focused on acquiring lands, not building facilities. However, design and construction accelerated during the Depression, when Iowa took rapid advantage of the New Deal's Emergency Conservation Work program, later renamed the Civilian Conservation Corps, to carry out—and expand on—earlier plans. Eventually, twenty-eight CCC camps were established in state parks across Iowa, each with hundreds of young men planting trees and constructing trails and buildings. Many of the projects the CCC crews built were designed by Fitzsimmons—who became Iowa's chief ECW landscape architect—

and an expanded team of designers. Working from a central design office located first in Ames and later in Des Moines, the team included recent landscape architecture graduates as well as other state and federal personnel and was largely, though not exclusively, funded by the National Park Service.

To keep the CCC workforce busy, the designers produced prodigious numbers of plans between 1931 and 1942. These included overall plans (renamed master plans under National Park Service and Emergency Conservation Work guidance), some for the twenty-two new state parks added in the late 1930s, as well as detailed designs for myriad recreational facilities. The team also produced a pattern book of standard furnishings such as benches, stairs, trails, campfire grills, and walls that CCC supervisors could adapt in the field on their own. Although such standardization increased during the seven years of CCC funding, the central office continued to produce singular designs that expressed a park's unique spirit of place, particularly for larger structures. One such example was the combined boat-bathhouse at Lake Wapello State Park. Designed by architect Amos B. Emery, the sprawling form of this idiosyncratic limestone building framed multiple views of the lake and beach. In some cases, higher-ups criticized the team for overdesigning projects beyond the abilities of the untrained CCC crews. However, based on the many structures that still stand in Iowa's parks eighty-plus years later, these concerns may have been exaggerated.

Indeed, the extensive and exemplary nature of Iowa's designed and constructed Civilian Conservation

Corps work was demonstrated when multiple projects were included in Albert H. Good's book *Park and Recreation Structures*. Published by the National Park Service in 1938, this manual of park design codified successful projects for other states to copy as they implemented their own parks. Along with a handful of other states, Iowa's park designs thus helped define the standards for a national style of park design that spread rapidly throughout the entire nation. Now known widely as park rustic design or parkitecture, this style of park design has achieved iconic status. For many citizens, a rustic log bench at the end of a winding stone-stepped trail and a cedar-shake shingled picnic shelter still define their expectations of an experience in nature. Perhaps this is why, despite a period after World War II when state park design moved to a form-follows-function Modern style of building, recent designs for Honey Creek Resort and

Banner Lakes at Summerset State Park feature stone-faced entry gates and half-timbered structures that recall traditional rustic architecture.

Today, Iowa's state parks retain a rich legacy of landscape architectural design. More than many other states, Iowa's parks preserve their historic road and trail layouts in addition to their significant CCC-era structures, and maintaining these now-historic features is an increasingly important part of park management. Yet the legacy of design is not just contained in physical structures; it is also contained in the ideas that built those structures: ideas about aesthetics and the balance between conservation and use. As our state parks transition into their second century, it's worth acknowledging that these ideas—comprehensive planning, respect for natural resources, and the desire to create places that rejuvenate the human spirit—are as worthy of celebration as the parks themselves.

# State Parks and State Recreation Areas

Iowa's 1917 State Park Act used the term "state park" to signify a place of exceptional value for its scientific, historic, or scenic interest. The quality of scientific interest included prairies, forests, and waters in their natural condition; native plants and animals; and caves, fossils, and other geologic features. Historic interest meant places associated with Euro-American exploration and settlement as well as archaeological sites, most notably burial mounds and artifacts associated with people who predated the arrival of Euro-Americans.

Recreation was not mentioned in the 1917 act, but members of the Iowa State Board of Conservation, the new agency charged with establishing and caring for state parks, quickly realized that the public at large thought of state parks primarily as places for outdoor recreation. Subsequent amendments to the act in 1919 and 1921 did not incorporate references to recreational values. However, the board's 1919 report quietly slipped "recreational interests" into the list of qualities

desirable in state parks. As the park system has evolved, recreational interests have assumed greater and greater value in the design and management of state parks.

This evolution is reflected in the various classification schemes applied to state parks over the decades. During the 1920s, the State Board of Conservation began giving different labels to some land acquisitions in order to highlight their scientific value as natural areas. In 1937, when park development was in full swing and after the State Board of Conservation merged with the Fish and Game Commission to become the Iowa Conservation Commission, the commission issued a booklet titled "Iowa's State Parks and Preserves." In it, the commission attempted to sort out the difference between state parks—"areas of state-wide rather than local interest, most widely known and used for varied scientific study and recreation"—and scientific preserves—"areas concerned with the protection and propagation of all forms of biological and botanical life and with the preservation of geologic features." However, many places did not fit neatly into these categories. When the commission formally adopted a classification scheme in 1941, it was a jumble of categories: state parks, recreation reserves, lake reserves, forest reserves, historical-archaeological monuments, geologic-biologic reserves, waysides, parkways, and "other" areas.

Clear distinctions finally began to emerge in 1963, when the commission reclassified the system into parks, recreation areas, and preserves. State parks were now defined as "relatively large areas of outstanding scenic or wilderness qualities" where recreational activities were not to interfere with resource preservation. State recreation areas were defined as "areas selected and developed primarily to provide outdoor recreation for more than local needs, but also having scenic qualities." Preserves were defined as small areas "established primarily to preserve objects of historic and scientific interest and places commemorating important persons or historic events." Two years later, the 1965 State Preserves Act codified a more precise definition. Since then, the "preserve" designation has been reserved for areas of "unusual flora, fauna, geological, archaeological, scenic or historic features of scientific or educational value."

This streamlined classification system was reaffirmed in 1986 when the Iowa Conservation Commission was combined with the Department of Water, Air and Waste Management to become the Iowa Department of Natural Resources. Separate bureaus were established to manage state parks and preserves, forests, and fish and wildlife areas. To visitors, however, these distinctions are not always evident. Sometimes state parks, recreation areas, and preserves exist together in one place—as is the case at Brushy Creek State Recreation Area and State Preserve—and sometimes state forests or wildlife management areas are adjacent—as is the case with Preparation Canyon State Park and the Loess Hills State Forest. Land classification is linked to management guidelines and priorities. In state parks, the goal is to provide amenities for outdoor recreation and, at the same time, to protect each site's natural, historic, and scenic qualities. State recreation areas accommodate more intensive recreational use, including hunting, as long as these activities do not stress the natural resource base.

Portrayed in this section are seventy-one state parks, eleven state recreation areas, five integrated state preserves, and two spots that have eluded classification—Galland School and Lake Odessa Campground. All these represent a particular moment in time. As Iowa's state park system enters its second century, the contributions of local governments and friends groups are becoming increasingly important. Currently, fourteen county conservation boards, one municipality, and one township board manage sixteen state parks. County conservation boards are also assuming greater responsibility for conservation education. Many counties have built nature centers, and almost all of them offer educational programs and field outings. Many cooperating community organizations have transitioned into park friends groups, several of which are featured at the end of this book. Working closely with park managers to support conservation efforts as well as public programs, these groups also use social media to organize volunteers, publicize events, and raise funds. We celebrate their accomplishments.

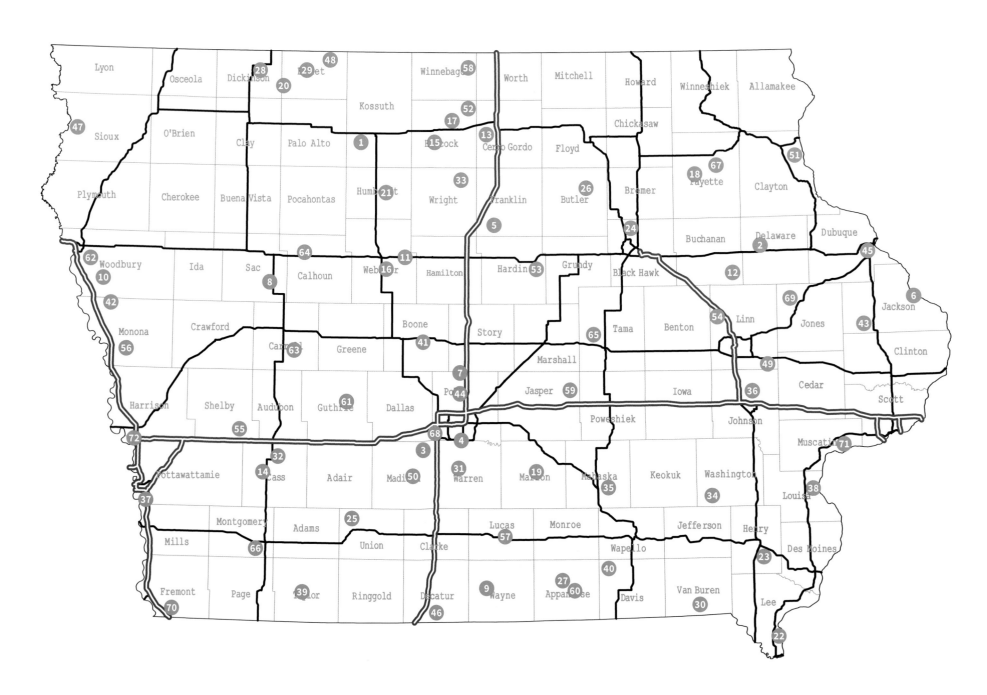

# State Parks and State Recreation Areas

1   Ambrose A. Call State Park
2   Backbone State Park
3   Badger Creek State Recreation Area
4   Banner Lakes at Summerset State Park
5   Beeds Lake State Park
6   Bellevue State Park
7   Big Creek State Park
8   Black Hawk State Park
9   Bobwhite State Park
10   Browns Lake–Bigelow Park
11   Brushy Creek State Recreation Area and State Preserve
12   Cedar Rock State Park
13   Clear Lake State Park | McIntosh Woods State Park
14   Cold Springs State Park
15   Crystal Lake State Park
16   Dolliver Memorial State Park
17   Eagle Lake State Park
18   Echo Valley State Park
19   Elk Rock State Park
20   Fort Defiance State Park
21   Frank A. Gotch State Park
22   Galland School
23   Geode State Park
24   George Wyth Memorial State Park
25   Green Valley State Park
26   Heery Woods State Park
27   Honey Creek State Park | Honey Creek Resort State Park

28   Iowa Great Lakes Region: Elinor Bedell State Park, Emerson Bay State Recreation Area, Gull Point State Park, Lower Gar State Recreation Area, Marble Beach State Recreation Area, Mini-Wakan State Park, Pikes Point State Park, Pillsbury Point State Park, Templar State Recreation Area, Trappers Bay State Park
29   Kearny State Park
30   Lacey-Keosauqua State Park
31   Lake Ahquabi State Park
32   Lake Anita State Park
33   Lake Cornelia State Park
34   Lake Darling State Park
35   Lake Keomah State Park
36   Lake Macbride State Park
37   Lake Manawa State Park
38   Lake Odessa Campground
39   Lake of Three Fires State Park
40   Lake Wapello State Park
41   Ledges State Park
42   Lewis and Clark State Park
43   Maquoketa Caves State Park
44   Margo Frankel Woods State Park
45   Mines of Spain State Recreation Area | Catfish Creek State Preserve
46   Nine Eagles State Park
47   Oak Grove State Park
48   Okamanpedan State Park
49   Palisades-Kepler State Park | Palisades-Dows State Preserve

50   Pammel State Park
51   Pikes Peak State Park
52   Pilot Knob State Park | Pilot Knob State Preserve
53   Pine Lake State Park
54   Pleasant Creek State Recreation Area
55   Prairie Rose State Park
56   Preparation Canyon State Park
57   Red Haw State Park
58   Rice Lake State Park
59   Rock Creek State Park
60   Sharon Bluffs State Park
61   Springbrook State Park
62   Stone State Park | Mount Talbot State Preserve
63   Swan Lake State Park
64   Twin Lakes State Park
65   Union Grove State Park
66   Viking Lake State Park
67   Volga River State Recreation Area
68   Walnut Woods State Park
69   Wapsipinicon State Park
70   Waubonsie State Park
71   Wildcat Den State Park | Fairport State Recreation Area
72   Wilson Island State Recreation Area

# Ambrose A. Call State Park

Ambrose A. Call State Park captures the ambitious spirit of pioneer settlers. In 1854, just three years after the last cession of Native American lands to the new state of Iowa, brothers Asa and Ambrose Call, born in Ohio, headed west. They wanted more than land to farm; they were aiming to establish a town. North of Fort Dodge, near the East Fork of the Des Moines River, they staked a claim and built a log cabin on what is now parkland. A bit farther north, they selected a town site, which they platted and named Algona, a word supposedly derived from Algonquian. Both brothers eventually acquired substantial landholdings and spent the rest of their lives promoting the settlement and growth of Algona and Kossuth County.

The 138-acre park bears Ambrose's name because of his oldest daughter, Florence. In 1884, she married Gardner Cowles, who had come to Algona to serve as superintendent of schools and soon thereafter went into banking with his father-in-law. Then, in 1903, newspaperman Harvey Ingham convinced Cowles to purchase the *Des Moines Register and Leader*, and the two men went on to build one of the finest newspapers in the country. In 1925, Florence Call Cowles donated this land to the state for a park in memory of her father.

The pioneer-era log cabin in the park is authentic, although it is not the 1854 cabin built by the Call brothers. In 1926, when the park was opened to the public, this cabin was moved to the park from the August Zahlten homestead. The park's distinctive peeled-log lodge, constructed in 1928 and restored in 1998 and 2019, is one of few surviving buildings

LELAND SEARLES

associated with the era of limited state park development in the 1920s. Both structures complement the park's heavily wooded terrain, a sharp contrast with the surrounding agricultural landscape.

"Algona" is also the name given to one of the major glacial moraines within the Des Moines Lobe landscape. This prominent ridge, which dips through five north-central Iowa counties, marks the accumulation of deposits around the edge of the last stand of glacial ice in Iowa about 12,000 years ago. The East Fork of the Des Moines River carves through these deposits.

# Backbone State Park

As early as the 1860s, naturalists were studying the geology and plant life of the Devil's Backbone area in Delaware County, so named for a steep and narrow dolomite ridge overlooking the Maquoketa River and belonging to the Silurian age of geologic time. Long before the State Park Act passed in 1917, there was talk of protecting this area. In 1896, geologist Samuel Calvin wrote, "The 'Backbone' is a fragment of unique topography that . . . preserves the characteristics of the pre-glacial surface of the State. . . . If it can only be let alone, it will remain a source of purest pleasure . . . where one may have direct contact with woods and rocks as Nature left them."

A recently completed twenty-year study documented more than 560 species of native vascular plants in the park, and the magnitude would have been just as great in the early twentieth century. It is thus no surprise that Backbone became Iowa's first state park. At its opening meeting on December 28, 1918, the Iowa State Board of Conservation recommended the purchase of at least 1,200 acres. In little more than a year, forty-four landowners had sold or donated land to the state for park purposes. On May 28, 1920, Governor W. L. Harding, flanked by members of the Board of Conservation and several politicians, dedicated the park before the "great concourse of people" who attended the ceremony.

Although land acquisition was the primary goal in the early years, the board authorized a number of improvements at Backbone during the 1920s. The construction of park roads began in 1923, and tree planting followed. In 1925, an existing barn was refashioned into a caretaker's lodge, and a new barn,

a trout hatchery complex, and stone entrance portals were built. A very large nature study complex was proposed for the north end of the park. However, only one building was constructed: an open-walled stone auditorium. Much of this work was done by inmates from Anamosa State Penitentiary. These features, which are still standing, represent the largest collection of state park improvements designed by landscape architect John R. Fitzsimmons and built before the expansive New Deal era.

Between 1933 and late 1941, two Civilian Conservation Corps crews were constantly at work in the park. In the southern area, they built a recreation area around a 125-acre artificial lake; more than two dozen cabins were added in the 1940s. The central area was developed for picnicking, hiking, and camping. In the northern area, CCC crews reconstructed the trout hatchery and built tranquil Richmond Springs, an artificially enhanced natural spring that feeds a trout stream. By 1942, at 1,415 acres,

CARL KURTZ, FACING PAGE: IOWA DNR

REECE THOMPSON

Backbone was considered Iowa's flagship park; it now covers 2,001 acres. Because of the exceptional quality of the approximately 125 structures built in the 1920s and 1930s, the whole park as it was constituted in 1942 is listed on the National Register of Historic Places.

In 1989, the caretaker's lodge was refashioned once again into a museum honoring the work of the Civilian Conservation Corps in Iowa's state parks. During the 1990s, the Iowa Department of Natural Resources repaired the CCC-constructed dam and dredged the lake, with volunteer assistance, converted the distinctive beach house into a day-use lodge, restored the classic boathouse and eight historic cabins, and built eight new cabins. Backbone State Forest sits adjacent to the park's northeast corner. This 186-acre tract, formerly farmland, was planted with a variety of pines to help protect the lake's watershed. Unlike the park, the state forest is open to hunting and horseback riding.

# Badger Creek State Recreation Area

Badger Creek State Recreation Area is an offshoot of the Badger Creek watershed project undertaken by the Soil Conservation Service and soil conservation districts in Madison, Dallas, and Warren Counties. In 1960, Congress approved and provided initial funding for the project, which covered more than 34,000 acres and was designed to control the flooding of farms in the Badger Creek floodplain. As the project evolved, especially its plans to create multiple water impoundments, Soil Conservation Service officials and the Iowa Conservation Commission began discussing the prospect of combining two of the planned impoundments to create a larger lake suitable for recreational use. The three local conservation districts supported this change, and thus, in 1964, the Iowa Conservation Commission decided to join the watershed project by helping finance the creation of a 276-acre lake. Such impoundments are common across southern Iowa, where old glacial plains are well drained and deeply creased. The hilly terrain creates many picturesque indentations along the shorelines.

Rising land costs and other land acquisition difficulties unfortunately delayed the project for many years. In 1980, when construction finally began on the dam to create Badger Creek Lake, plans for recreational facilities were scaled down because, in the intervening years, significant water-related recreational amenities had been developed at nearby Saylorville Lake and Big Creek State Park. At Badger Creek, the Iowa Conservation Commission now focused on creating fish and wildlife habitats and facilitating low-impact recreational uses. The lake is now a popular fishing spot, and the surrounding

KEVIN KANE

recreation area, which covers more than 700 acres, is open to public hunting.

VIC KESSE

# Banner Lakes at Summerset State Park

Behind its elegant name, Banner Lakes at Summerset reveals a striking transformation of an industrial landscape. The name Banner refers to the Banner Coal Company, and the lakes are former open-pit coal mines. From the 1870s to the early 1940s, coal mining was part of Warren County's economy; about a dozen companies operated in the Summerset area at one time or another. The Banner/Evansville Strip Mine at Summerset—said to have been the largest strip mine in Iowa—opened in 1932 but operated for less than a decade. Because the four-foot seam of Pennsylvanian age coal was located just 40 feet below the surface, strip mining was the only feasible way to extract it. When the company closed in the late 1930s, the abandoned mine filled with water and became known as Banner Pits.

In 1954, the Iowa Conservation Commission purchased the property for use as a wildlife management area. However, as the recreational needs of the Des Moines metropolitan area grew and changed, many people began to eye the pits as attractive sites for more diverse outdoor activities. After several years of planning, Banner Pits became Banner Lakes, Iowa's newest state park, dedicated in 2004. In addition to fishing and no-wake boating, the 222-acre park has more than 5 miles of multiple-use trails. Mountain bike trails offer three levels of challenge through parts of this unusual reclaimed landscape, and a bike loop through the park connects it with the Summerset Trail, a 12-mile paved rail trail from Carlisle to Indianola. A supervised shooting range is located along the park's eastern edge. The park sits adjacent to the thousand-

JIM SCHEFFLER

acre Banner Flats Wildlife Management Area, where public hunting is allowed.

DON POGGENSEE

# Beeds Lake State Park

Beeds Lake is named for William Beed, who operated a mill in this location from 1864 until 1903. Spring Creek, first formed as a meltwater stream draining the eastern edge of the Des Moines Lobe ice front, was dammed as early as 1857 to power a sawmill, and a flour mill was added two years later. Both were essential elements of pioneer settlements in the nineteenth century, but railroads and good roads eventually made local mills unnecessary. Beed's Mill was torn down in 1916, and the millpond was drained.

During the 1920s, the Izaak Walton League became a powerful conservation organization, promoting fair play among anglers and working to save waterways and wildlife. In Iowa, the league promoted the construction of artificial fishing lakes, which ultimately led to the creation of Beeds Lake State Park. In 1933, the league's local chapter took the lead in helping the city of Hampton purchase 254 acres, which included the site of Beed's Mill. The city, in turn, gave the land to the state for the creation of a lake and park.

Between 1934, when the park opened, and 1938, Civilian Conservation Corps workers transformed the old mill site into a scenic lake park. Prominent structures—listed on the National Register of Historic Places—include a rustic stone-and-timber bathhouse, now a day-use lodge, and a striking limestone spillway that creates a misty waterfall effect when water tumbles down its stepped wall. The 319-acre park is a popular camping, picnicking, fishing, and swimming spot. Surrounding the lake is a 2-mile walking and biking trail that crosses a long

causeway separating the lake from the old millpond. The causeway provides excellent shoreline fishing.

# Bellevue State Park

Stand quietly on the Silurian age dolomite bluff towering 250 feet above the magnificent Mississippi River valley. The sight says it all: *belle vue*. The name, however, is a clever play on words, for the town below, from which the park takes its name, was platted in 1835 by John Bell. Still, the view belongs to the ages. That's what citizens of Bellevue thought in 1908, when they created a park commission and started planning to preserve the bluff. After passage of the 1917 State Park Act, a state park became the goal. In 1925, the park commission sold the first of several parcels to the state for park purposes. Inmates from Anamosa State Penitentiary were assigned to improve the park with roads and signs, picnic shelters, a nine-hole golf course, and a peeled-log lodge.

In addition to preserving the view for posterity, the park also protects undated Native American mounds as well as the remains of a nineteenth-century lime kiln and its related quarry. However, there have been many changes over the years. In the 1960s, the state purchased a 300-acre tract 2 miles south of the original park. This area, which also overlooks the river, became the Dyas Unit, named for the land seller, Wilbur J. Dyas. Eventually, the Dyas Unit was developed with a campground as well as picnic shelters and viewing areas. Land has also been added to the original park, and in 1970 the northern area was named the Nelson Unit. The name honors Lawrence Nelson, a local Presbyterian minister who served on the Iowa Conservation Commission in the 1960s and was instrumental in securing the Dyas Unit. In the late 1990s, the state added a 224-

KEN FORMANEK

acre tract to the Nelson Unit for public hunting use. Today's park encompasses 788 acres.

After fire destroyed the historic lodge in 1975, it was replaced with a new lodge constructed of western red cedar. In 1984, the golf clubhouse was converted into the South Bluff Nature Center, and a small portion of the former golf course was transformed into a butterfly garden with a universally accessible sidewalk. Community volunteers tend the garden, which attracts more than sixty species of butterflies.

# Big Creek State Park

Big Creek's story is tied to that of Saylorville Reservoir. In the 1930s, the U.S. Army Corps of Engineers began a multidecade initiative to construct high flood-control dams on many of the nation's rivers. High dams conveniently produced large artificial lakes that could be used for outdoor recreation. Saylorville, which dammed the Des Moines River above the city of Des Moines, was first proposed in 1939, but construction did not begin until 1965. Big Creek Reservoir, a companion to Saylorville, was built in 1971 and 1972 to protect Polk City from flooding.

In the mid-1960s, Iowa embarked on its own large lakes program to create artificial lakes for outdoor recreation near urban centers. Saylorville and Big Creek Reservoirs, as federal projects, were already set to provide two large lakes for the Des Moines metro area. Correspondingly, a 1967 legislative appropriation for outdoor recreation earmarked $1 million for land acquisition to create a state park near Big Creek. This project was handed to the Iowa Conservation Commission along with another legislatively approved project to create Hawkeye Naturama near Polk City. Its Disneyland-like concept—promoted as conservation education for everyone with features such as a Hall of Prehistoric Animals and a meditation garden—simply dumbfounded commissioners.

By the time Big Creek Lake filled, in 1972, the fantastical Hawkeye Naturama concept had faded away. Land adjacent to the lake was developed with a beach complex, boat-launch ramps, and picnic shelters, much like the state's other lake parks. The 3,550-acre park is now complemented by Big Creek Wildlife Management Area and a multiple-use

downstream corridor extending to Des Moines, both of which are open to seasonal hunting. Recreation amenities have expanded to include a marina concession, a universally accessible fishing pier, twenty-two rental shelters, and a large playground. For bicyclists and hikers, the park is linked to Des Moines by a 26-mile paved, multiple-use trail that provides access to a much larger network of trails.

# Black Hawk State Park

First called Boyer Lake, then Wall Lake, this 957-acre natural lake was renamed Black Hawk as part of extensive development in the 1950s. A local physician, Everett E. Speaker, who served on the Iowa Conservation Commission from 1935 to 1956, played a key role by helping the state acquire several parcels of land adjacent to the lake, which provided public access at three different points. This continued a 1920s community effort to acquire shorefront property within the town of Lake View to create a municipal park overlooking the lake on the west side.

Crews from two Civilian Conservation Corps camps provided the labor for development. The largest parcel, which contained a long gravel pit that had filled with water, was named Lake Arrowhead. It was planted with trees and turned into a wildlife refuge with hiking trails and fish-rearing ponds. Park headquarters buildings and a stone overlook were constructed here. Stone-and-log picnic shelters were built at the other two access points: Thirty Acres on the southeast shore and Denison Beach on the north shore.

While these three state-owned areas were being developed, CCC crews were assigned to further develop the municipal park with two distinctive stone piers. Additionally, the community, again assisted by Dr. Speaker, arranged for the School of Fine Arts at the University of Iowa to create a statue of Black Hawk, the famous Sauk war chief. Designed by sculptor Harry E. Stinson, the cast-stone statue was unveiled at an elaborate lake-renaming ceremony on September 3, 1934. The CCC-built park structures and Chief Black Hawk statue are listed on the National Register of Historic Places.

DON POGGENSEE

Black Hawk Lake is a glacial lake formed as melting took place along the western margin of the Des Moines Lobe about 13,000 years ago. It is a very popular boating, camping, and fishing spot, and the 33-mile Sauk Rail Trail connects the 275-acre park with Swan Lake State Park in Carroll County. The lake's extensive watershed is only partially protected by the wildlife refuge and a larger wildlife management area. To help maintain water quality and healthy fish populations, the lake has been dredged multiple times. Since 2014, a group of citizens, the Black Hawk Lake Protective Association, has assisted the Iowa Department of Natural Resources' efforts.

# Bobwhite State Park

The backstory of Bobwhite State Park is one of the more unusual of Iowa's parks. Until 1962, the site was known as Allerton Reservoir, constructed in 1912 and 1913 by the Chicago, Rock Island and Pacific Railroad near the town of Allerton to provide water for its operations. In 1945, the Iowa Conservation Commission entertained an idea to purchase the reservoir for a nominal sum in order to add a ready-made artificial lake in Wayne County. The reservoir was already a popular fishing spot, and state ownership would help advance the Iowa Twenty-five Year Conservation Plan's goal of providing all Iowans with easy access to a lake park. It took two years to negotiate a land purchase deal, but in 1947 the state acquired 551 acres, including the reservoir, with the railroad retaining the right to draw water for as long as needed.

The reservoir impounds waters of the South Fork of the Chariton River to create a finger lake in a steeply sloping valley. Such deep valleys, characteristic of southern Iowa landscapes, are carved into glacial plains older than 500,000 years that are mantled with windblown loess. Between 1949 and the mid-1950s, Wayne County built a road to the park, and the Iowa Conservation Commission created a swimming beach and picnic areas, planted walnut trees, and made improvements to the dam and spillway. However, the ICC never got around to renaming Allerton Reservoir. This oversight was rectified in 1962 when the Wayne County Chamber of Commerce sponsored a naming contest. The winning entry was Bobwhite State Park. It is Iowa's only state park named for a particular species of wildlife, the

MISSOURI DEPARTMENT OF CONSERVATION

northern bobwhite, which also happens to be the only quail species found in Iowa.

In 2002, the Wayne County Conservation Board assumed park management under an agreement with the Iowa Department of Natural Resources. Since then, the county conservation board has improved campground facilities, picnic areas, and the 5-mile trail system that winds through 15 acres of restored prairie. Future improvements will make key areas of the park and lake, now 390 acres in size, universally accessible.

# Browns Lake–Bigelow Park

Browns Lake may take its name from Brown's Settlement, a community in its vicinity that had a brief life in the 1850s and early 1860s. Both the lake and the settlement may have been named for John W. Brown, one of the earliest settlers in Woodbury County. In any case, the lake had been so named by 1868, when the first local history was penned. At that time, Browns Lake was reported as "fast drying up," as were two other oxbow lakes in the area. All three lakes formed when the meandering Missouri River changed course and stranded sections of its former channel.

Browns Lake, however, was large enough that it did not dry up, and in the late 1930s the Iowa Conservation Commission riprapped the shoreline extensively to stop erosion. The state also purchased a large island in the lake and planted it for wildlife habitat. After sports lovers began advocating for a state park, the ICC acquired 36 acres on the south shore in 1946, land that had once been owned by another pioneer settler, A. T. Bigelow. The park, which primarily provided public access to the lake for fishing and boating, was minimally developed with picnic and camping facilities. In the early 1960s, the Woodbury County Chapter of the Izaak Walton League took a special interest in the park and lake, became a vocal champion for improving both, and maintained a clubhouse in the park for many years.

In 1970, the Woodbury County Conservation Board assumed management of Bigelow Park under an agreement with the Conservation Commission. In the following years, the county conservation board developed the park with paved roads, a new bathhouse and concession building, modern camping facilities,

LELAND SEARLES

playground equipment, enclosed picnic shelters, a new boat ramp, and a supervised swimming beach. The Iowa Department of Natural Resources continues to manage the 580-acre lake as well as Browns Lake Wildlife Management Area, the large island in the center of the lake.

IOWA DNR

# Brushy Creek State Recreation Area and State Preserve

Iowa's largest park also lays claim to being the most controversial in its establishment. Local interest in a lake-based park surfaced in the mid-1960s, when the state began creating a series of large lake parks near urban areas. After intense lobbying by business and civic leaders persuaded the Iowa Conservation Commission to investigate feasible sites near Fort Dodge, Brushy Creek became one of three projects approved by the legislature in 1967. However, land acquisition proceeded slowly, and water-quality issues further delayed development.

The commission opened Brushy Creek to recreational use as parcels were acquired, beginning in 1968, while it debated how to control pollution in the watershed of the proposed lake. Meanwhile, equestrians, hikers, hunters, mountain bikers, bird watchers, and other outdoor enthusiasts began to establish use patterns that did not depend on the presence of a lake. Organized environmental groups also took an interest in the project and began promoting a multiple-use recreation area with no lake. An environmental study completed in 1982 documented a wide range of public opinion concerning the desired level of development. Equally important, the study identified surviving patches of native prairie and woodland, several rare and endangered animal species, dozens of American Indian archaeological sites, and important records of Iowa's glacial history in the park's landscapes and underlying deposits. The combination of competing user interests and new information about vulnerable plants, animals, and cultural sites led to more debate and indecision. Recreational use continued, however, and increased.

LARRY STONE

The project was revived in 1986, and a new development plan, approved by the Natural Resources Commission in 1988, featured a 690-acre lake to the north and a vast network of multiple-use trails. At that time, 260 acres were dedicated as a geological, archaeological, and biological state preserve. To compensate for the loss of existing trails in the proposed lake area, the legislature approved the acquisition of additional land. The legislature also established an advisory board to assist the Iowa Department of Natural Resources with future trail development.

The new plan, which carefully balanced outdoor recreation values with environmental concerns, did not please everyone. However, it reflected a coherent management philosophy that satisfied most of the people who had a stake in Brushy Creek's development. Construction of the dam began in 1995, and the lake was dedicated in 1998. Brushy Creek covers 6,500 acres and offers extensive modern camping facilities, including two equestrian campgrounds, 45 miles of multiple-use trails, target ranges, picnic areas, fishing jetties, boat ramps, and a swimming beach.

# Cedar Rock State Park

Visitors to Cedar Rock may wonder why an architectural masterpiece is a state park. The straightforward answer is that Lowell and Agnes Walter, who commissioned renowned architect Frank Lloyd Wright to design a three-season home after they retired in 1944, arranged to donate this part of their estate to the people of Iowa when they could no longer use it. After Lowell died in 1981, Agnes donated an 11-acre parcel containing the house and boathouse to the Iowa Conservation Commission. The buildings are listed on the National Register of Historic Places.

The less obvious answer is that Cedar Rock, named for a limestone promontory overlooking the Wapsipinicon River, exemplifies Wright's talent for harmonizing buildings with their natural settings. Wright drew design inspiration from midwestern landscapes, and many of his buildings dot the Midwest. Of the ten in Iowa, Cedar Rock is the most complete, meaning that the furniture and furnishings which Wright also designed are still there. So are the entrance portals, an outdoor entertainment terrace, and Wright's tile signature, which he applied only to places he considered special. This may be why the Walters, who had no children, wanted the people of Iowa to enjoy this place in perpetuity.

Cedar Rock, preserved just as they left it, is open for tours from mid-May to mid-October. Until 2009, the buildings and grounds were maintained in partnership with the Walter Charitable Trust Fund. During that time, the trust fund purchased an additional 185 acres, and a visitor center was constructed on a portion of the addition in the early 1990s. In 2010, a nonprofit group, the Friends of

Cedar Rock, formed to raise nearly $200,000 needed to restore the boathouse. Their contribution to the restoration, completed in 2017, was recognized with a Governor's Volunteer Award in 2018. The friends group continues to assist the Iowa Department of Natural Resources with preservation, public programs, and tours.

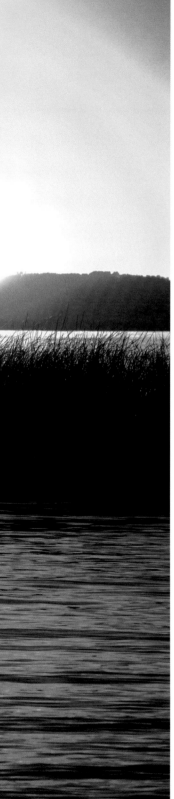

# Clear Lake State Park | McIntosh Woods State Park

Clear Lake, at 3,625 acres, is the main attraction of these two small state parks. Of glacial origin, it is situated along the eastern edge of the Des Moines Lobe's icy advance into north-central Iowa between 15,000 and 12,000 years ago. Natural lakes and waterways are part of Iowa's sovereign lands, but these waters were surrounded by privately owned lands long before the state park system was established. A large town grew along the eastern shore, and a smaller town, Ventura, was established on the northern shore. Thus, the area around Clear Lake was well populated. The initial challenge, then, was to provide adequate public access to public waters.

Clear Lake State Park, acquired in the mid-1920s, is a 55-acre site on the southeastern shore. It is almost fully developed with a beach 900 feet long, extensive picnic grounds, a modern campground, and a playground. An impressive stone-and-timber lodge for large gatherings, constructed in 1938 by local workers hired through the Works Progress Administration, was completely renovated in 1999.

In 1937, a group of local citizens organized the Association for the Preservation of Clear Lake to help address water-quality problems. After successfully pressing for a sanitary sewer system around the lake, the association began to lobby for more public shoreline. The result was McIntosh Woods State Park, a 60-acre site on the lake's northwestern shore, which the Iowa Conservation Commission purchased in 1943 from Rose McIntosh. The park provides the major boat-launch point for the lake as well as fishing

IOWA DNR

jetties, picnic grounds, playgrounds, modern camping facilities, two rental yurts for a cabin experience, a wildlife-viewing boardwalk and blind, and a bike trail.

The association was also instrumental in acquiring Ventura Marsh Wildlife Management Area, which surrounds the western reaches of the lake. Between 2008 and 2015, the Iowa Department of Natural Resources, with federal and local assistance, undertook a series of lake restoration efforts. These included dredging 2.4 million cubic yards of sediment from the Little Lake portion of Clear Lake and riprapping 1,500 feet of shoreline with native stone. The lake restoration project substantially improved the water quality in both the lake and the marsh.

# Cold Springs State Park

Once known as Crystal Lake, this spot has been a local gathering place for more than a century. In 1896, landowner D. W. Woodward dug a small lake in a wooded area of his farm, filled it with water piped from a large spring that flowed from a nearby bluff along the Nishnabotna River, and developed a summer resort. According to various reports, the hilly resort had a swimming beach with diving boards and a waterslide, a picnic area with a pavilion and concession stand, a baseball field, and a skating rink. Rental boats were available, and tent camping was allowed on "the hill."

After the Nishnabotna was rechannelized in the mid-1920s, the lake began to dry up—just as public demand for lake-based recreation began to rise. Adoption of the Iowa Twenty-five Year Conservation Plan in 1933, which called for the construction of many artificial lakes, mainly in southern Iowa, stimulated residents of Cass County to raise money to purchase a 60-acre tract containing Crystal Lake, which Woodward was willing to sell. In 1938, the tract was donated to the state for park purposes. The Iowa Conservation Commission initially considered enlarging the lake, which was renamed Cold Springs (presumably to avoid confusion with Crystal Lake in Hancock County). In actuality, though, very few improvements were made until 1949, when work began on reconstructing the existing 16-acre lake, which reopened in 1951.

Ten years later, in 1961, the Cass County Conservation Board assumed park management under an agreement with the Iowa Conservation

ERIK ROWLEY

Commission; the board later added an enclosed picnic shelter. Cold Springs State Park, now 104 acres in size, continues to be a popular spot for swimming, fishing, boating, and picnicking. Cass County Conservation Board offices are located in the park, as is a regional Iowa Department of Natural Resources fisheries station.

# Crystal Lake State Park

Crystal Lake in Hancock County is one of many lakes that were left across north-central Iowa when the Des Moines Lobe ice advanced, then melted, 15,000 to 12,000 years ago. Pioneer settlers drained shallower lakes for farmland, but the depth of Crystal Lake, 16 to 18 feet in the center, assured its survival. In 1902, Thomas Macbride noted that the lake's "clear surface invites the pleasure-seeker's boat," and a 1916 survey reported that the local community, which was "justly proud of this beautiful little sheet of water," had petitioned the Iowa State Board of Conservation to purchase land on its shores. By 1921, Crystal Lake was among dozens of areas under consideration for park development, but land acquisition was delayed until the 1950s.

Park development was finally initiated by local citizens. In the mid-1950s, the Crystal Lake Commercial Club obtained a lease on a 15-acre tract known as Ellsworth College Park on the east side of the 264-acre lake. In 1958, the lease was transferred to the newly organized Hancock County Conservation Board. Then in 1969, the Iowa Conservation Commission purchased about 150 acres along the shore, which included the leased acres, and entered into a new management lease that authorized the county board to "develop the land as it saw fit."

The park, which now covers about 25 acres, is well developed with modern and nonmodern camping facilities, three modern cabins, a picnic and playground area, a small swimming beach, and a boat launch. The county board also manages a portion of the Crystal Lake Wildlife Management Area, which protects the watershed on the northeast shore and the uplands on the north side of the lake.

# Dolliver Memorial State Park

With geological features named Boneyard Hollow and Copperas Beds, Dolliver Memorial State Park justly invites exploration. Local citizens supported the Iowa State Board of Conservation's desire to establish a state park here, donating $10,000 from the Dolliver Memorial Fund toward the initial land purchase in 1921. To recognize this generosity, the park commemorates Jonathan Prentiss Dolliver, who served Iowa in the U.S. House of Representatives from 1889 to 1900, then in the U.S. Senate until his death in 1910. Noted sculptor Lorado Taft created the bronze tablet that memorializes Dolliver. In 1933, Civilian Conservation Corps workers constructed the naturalistic rock ledges above the tablet as well as the stone wall of the spring-fed pool in front of it.

The 617-acre park is rich in natural and cultural history. Its scenic landscape is heavily wooded, primarily with upland oak-dominated forests, but interspersed with prairie openings and wetlands. More than four hundred vascular plant species and several species of mosses and lichens occur in the park. Native American mounds associated with the Woodland period (800 BC–AD 1250) are located in the forested uplands. The awe-inspiring sandstone cliffs along the Des Moines River and its tributaries expose sequential layers of Pennsylvanian age sediments once deposited along ancient river channels. At the south end of the park, the cliffs line a former riverbed now known as Prairie Creek, which flows into the Des Moines River. Early geologists identified the greenish crystalline mineral deposits in the sandstone walls as ferrous sulfate or copperas. Later chemical analyses correctly identified the mineral as melanterite, but the name

Copperas Beds stuck. Boneyard Hollow, a beautiful cliff-lined ravine at the north end of the park, was named by pioneer settlers for the abundance of bison, elk, and deer bones found there, apparently animals hunted by Native Americans.

A caretaker's cabin and a lodge, both of log construction, were erected in the 1920s but dismantled in the 1930s when the park was extensively developed by Civilian Conservation Corps and Works Progress Administration crews. In addition to the Dolliver Memorial, several 1930s rustic stone-and-timber structures now constitute a National Register of Historic Places district within the park; these were renovated in the 1990s. The structures include the entrance portals, a round check-in station, a footbridge, two lodges, and two stone rental cabins. In recent years, the Iowa Department of Natural Resources has installed modern facilities at the campground and group camp, rebuilt trails as well as the ford across Prairie Creek, and upgraded the boat ramp and parking area on the Des Moines River.

# Eagle Lake State Park

Eagle Lake in Hancock County, not to be confused with Eagle Lake in Emmet County, has little open water, although its meandering boundary defines a marshy "lake" of about 900 acres within a wetland complex of more than 1,200 acres. During the early twentieth century, marshes and ponds extended north of the natural glacial lake for about 10 miles. One local observer noted that when he came to the area in 1900, many birds resided there or stopped during their annual migrations, and "ducks nested there in thousands." Thanks to the action of local residents in the 1920s, Eagle Lake is still a birder's paradise.

For many years, the William Ward family, who owned the tract that is now parkland, allowed people to cross their land to hunt and fish on the lake. Bert Bailey, a zoologist at Coe College in Cedar Rapids, spent summers with the Wards studying and collecting birds. The Wards' generosity seems to have cultivated local appreciation for the lake. In 1923, a group of citizens raised enough money to purchase 13 acres, which was the seed for a state park. This donation of land along with a subsequent land trade negotiated by the state resulted in a 21-acre state park. Local citizens then pitched in to help improve the park for picnicking and access to the lake for boating and fishing.

The Hancock County Conservation Board has managed the park since 1965. Today, the lake is part of a 1,270-acre wetland complex that includes parkland, a wildlife refuge, a nature area, and a wildlife management area that is open to seasonal hunting. A boardwalk and observation deck at the park allow visitors to observe marsh wildlife unobtrusively.

WARREN TERPSTRA

# Echo Valley State Park

Echo Valley State Park is named for the echo that reverberates in the deepest part of the park's narrow valley when someone shouts a loud "hello." Actually, two valleys conjoin in the park, carved by the waters of Otter Creek and Glover Creek (formerly Skunk Creek), which left a high narrow ridge between them known as the backbone region in central Fayette County. The park contains impressive, nearly vertical exposures of weathered Silurian age limestone that lines the creeks, creating a landscape of rugged bluffs and picturesque ledges.

County residents came together in 1934 to raise money for creating a state park in this scenic area. One of those residents was Grace Gilmore King, who served on the Iowa State Board of Conservation from 1932 to 1934. With this local contribution, the state purchased 107 acres, which included the site of a nineteenth-century gristmill and a lime kiln along Glover Creek. The latter reportedly was used to make lime for the mortar that Civilian Conservation Corps workers used in constructing a large stone-and-timber picnic shelter.

County employees and workers hired through the Works Progress Administration built a road through the park, planted pine trees, and constructed a dam for a small lake. In 1938 and 1939, the Echo Valley Chapter of the Future Farmers of America planted hardwood trees supplied by the state nursery. Unfortunately, the lake silted in rather quickly and was eventually drained. However, in the 1940s, the Iowa Conservation Commission began stocking trout in the cold waters of Glover and Otter Creeks. A railroad line through the park operated until midcentury.

Since 1986, the park has been managed by the Fayette County Conservation Board under an agreement with the Iowa Department of Natural Resources. The historic shelter was renovated in 1996, and a smaller shelter was added to the picnic area. In 2001, the park was enlarged to nearly 300 acres when the state purchased a tract of former pastureland on both sides of Glover Creek to improve water quality for trout fishing. The park also features a 2.5-mile multiple-use trail along the old railroad right-of-way, which was purchased by a private party in 2001 and developed with footbridges supported by the stone piers of the old railroad bridges.

# Elk Rock State Park

Elk Rock State Park developed along with Lake Red Rock, the largest of four multiple-use reservoirs created by U.S. Army Corps of Engineers flood-control projects in Iowa. Red Rock was created between 1960 and 1969 by damming the Des Moines River below the city of Des Moines. The valleys of its tributaries filled to form a 15,000-acre lake in steeply rolling terrain, a characteristic of the older well-drained glacial plains across southern Iowa. Reddish sandstone outcroppings of Pennsylvanian age are seen at a number of places along the shoreline. The 997-acre state park, situated on the south side of the lake, is part of a federal-state-county recreation complex that includes Cordova and Roberts Creek Parks, managed by the Marion County Conservation Board, and five recreation areas developed by the Corps of Engineers.

The Iowa Conservation Commission began developing facilities at the park in 1970, when two boat launches were opened. That year, the park was named Elk Rock for a prominent sandstone cliff on the south shore. The ICC also began constructing park offices and staff housing, access roads, and picnic areas. Further park development lagged, however, due to unusually high water in the lake during the first few years. In 1973, the first picnic shelter was constructed. Park amenities now include two campgrounds, one of them for equestrians, 13 miles of multiple-use trails that wind through a variety of habitats, two boat ramps, and two day-use picnic areas with open shelters. Paddling along the lakeshore beneath the cliffs is a popular activity for kayakers.

The Iowa Department of Natural Resources also manages the 31,000-acre Lake Red Rock Wildlife

JOHN PEARSON

Management Area, which provides habitat for more than two hundred species of birds and is a destination for viewing migratory waterfowl in spring and fall.

# Fort Defiance State Park

Fort Defiance was associated with the violent incidents of 1857 known as the Spirit Lake Massacre and the U.S.-Dakota War of 1862, which ushered in nearly three decades of warfare between federal troops and American Indian peoples throughout the western United States. This was the last phase of a long process spurred by the Indian Removal Act of 1830, a sad chapter of history that has been told mainly from the victors' point of view. Between 1857 and 1863, about a dozen forts were built in northwestern Iowa to garrison troops with the Iowa Northern Border Brigade and provide safe havens for white settlers. The crisis, however, was short-lived. Fort Defiance, built during the winter of 1862–63, was abandoned when the brigade disbanded in January 1864. Local residents dismantled the fortifications and reused the materials.

When wooded land near Estherville was acquired for a state park, it was named to memorialize this episode of Iowa's military history (the actual historic site lies within the city limits of Estherville). In the early 1930s, the city assisted the Iowa State Board of Conservation with park development by hiring unemployed men to build trails and construct a park lodge in the style of log fortifications built on the frontier in the nineteenth century. The lodge was repaired and modernized in 2001. Continuing the tradition of community involvement, since 2006 the Friends of Fort Defiance State Park have assisted the Iowa Department of Natural Resources in maintaining the 221-acre park's picnic areas, camping facilities, and 9 miles of multiple-use trails. In 2008, students at Iowa Lakes Community College raised funds for

LELAND SEARLES

and constructed an interpretive kiosk. Recently, the Friends and Iowa Lakes Community College collaborated to build an interpretive trail.

# Frank A. Gotch State Park

In 1942, just after the United States entered World War II, the Iowa Conservation Commission acquired the site of an early nineteenth-century trading post at the confluence of the east and west forks of the Des Moines River in Humboldt County. Park development was suspended for the duration of the war, but in the interim residents of Humboldt and Dakota City began to petition the ICC to name the new state park in honor of their most famous son, Frank A. Gotch, who held the World Heavyweight Wrestling Championship from 1908 to 1913. It seemed fitting because Gotch, who died in 1917, had grown up on a farm across the river from the new park. The ICC was not receptive, but the legislature was: it passed a joint resolution in 1949 to approve the name.

In 1952, the Humboldt–Dakota City Joint Chamber of Commerce obtained a ten-year lease on the park and began to develop it for recreational use. The chamber also erected a pink granite memorial to Gotch in the park. Ten years later, in 1962, the ICC transferred park management to the Humboldt County Conservation Board.

In addition to providing access to the river for boating and fishing, the 67-acre park is well developed with modern and nonmodern camping facilities, picnic areas, shelter houses, and a playground. Three Rivers Trail, a 40-mile multiple-use trail connecting the towns of Rolfe and Eagle Grove, runs through the park.

LELAND SEARLES

# Galland School

Although this Lee County schoolhouse is a replica of the original building and is not located on its original site, Galland School is an important touchstone for two related threads of Iowa history: education and pioneer entrepreneurship.

Isaac Galland (1791–1858), the school's namesake, came to Iowa amid the first wave of frontier settlers. Biographical details of his early life are sketchy, but clearly he was restless and ambitious. He grew up in Ohio, attended Ohio University, married twice, left both wives, then moved to Indiana Territory, where he studied and practiced medicine. In 1826, he pushed farther westward, to the eastern bank of the Mississippi River, where he established a trading post at present-day Oquawka, Illinois. By now, he had married a third time and started a family. Two years later, he sold the trading post and moved to the western side of the river, where he founded a settlement called Nashville, later renamed Galland.

In 1830, he built a 10-by-12 split-log schoolhouse and hired a teacher to educate his two young children and those of other settlers. The school, however, was short-lived: Galland moved his family back to the Illinois side of the river in 1832. He spent the rest of his life dealing in real estate on both sides of the river, promoting immigration, and (unsuccessfully) running for office in both Illinois and Iowa. The abandoned schoolhouse was repurposed for one use or another until, eventually, it was dismantled and used for firewood. When the dam near Keokuk was constructed in 1913, even the school site disappeared, submerged by the impoundment.

All that remained was the memory of Galland

School as Iowa's first formal school, which the Keokuk Chapter of the Daughters of the American Revolution commemorated in 1924 by placing a marker near the original schoolhouse location. In 1926, Timothy J. and Ella T. Harrington donated the commemoration site to the Iowa State Board of Conservation. To interpret the site, a replica schoolhouse was constructed in 1943. When this building deteriorated, a second replica was constructed in 1977. In 1986, the Lee County Conservation Department assumed management of the site under an agreement with the Iowa Department of Natural Resources and constructed a small amphitheater for interpretive programs.

JOHN PEARSON

# Geode State Park

This park takes its name from the crystal-lined, earth-shaped rocks that occur in far southeastern Iowa along tributaries of the Des Moines River. Here, creeks and rivers cut through loess-mantled glacial deposits to expose underlying outcrops of Mississippian age limestone and shale, in which geodes—Iowa's state rock—are found. Like a number of other state parks, Geode came about through local efforts. In this case, residents of Henry and Des Moines Counties purchased a steeply wooded 143-acre tract near the South Skunk River, a place long used as a picnic area, and offered it to the Iowa Conservation Commission in 1937 for a state park.

Between 1939 and 1942, Civilian Conservation Corps workers cleared trees, built roads, constructed a stone picnic shelter, and began constructing a park residence and maintenance building. After the Civilian Conservation Corps was disbanded in 1942, the Iowa Conservation Commission finished the latter two buildings. The ICC also began acquiring more land and studied the feasibility of creating an artificial lake. In 1947, when the legislature appropriated funds for the construction of additional lakes, Geode State Park was selected as one of the locations. A dam impounding the waters of Cedar Creek, a tributary of the South Skunk River, was completed in 1950. Additional park development followed, some of it accomplished by incarcerated workers after the ICC established a prison labor program in 1955. Work camps were located in four state parks, including Geode, where inmates constructed a CCC-like beach house as well as picnic tables, camp grills, signs, and such for use

IOWA GEOLOGICAL SURVEY

throughout the system. For a time in the 1950s, the park also had an airstrip.

The park now covers 1,641 acres, including the 174-acre lake. Amenities include a large modern campground, a youth group camping area, boat ramps, a swimming beach, and five picnic shelters—including the historic CCC shelter, recently restored. Seven miles of multiple-use trails loop around the lake, through oak and hickory uplands, and across restored prairie areas. Geode Lake, which is prone to siltation, has been the target of recent federal-state-local efforts to improve the watershed. In 2018, much of the park was closed while the lake was drained to remove accumulated silt, park facilities were upgraded, and the campground was renovated. The 46-mile Southeast Iowa Bike Route connects Geode and Lacey-Keosauqua State Parks via paved and lightly traveled county highways.

# George Wyth Memorial State Park

George Wyth, cofounder of the Viking Pump Company in Cedar Falls, philanthropist, and park advocate, would scarcely recognize the state park that bears his name, although it embodies the attributes he valued. Wyth conceived the idea for a state parkway along the Cedar River while serving on the Iowa State Board of Conservation from 1927 to 1933, but it was 1938 before a plan began to come together. At that time, the state obtained the first options for parkland, which included Fisher Lake, an old channel of the Cedar River. The planned scenic parkway between the sister cities of Cedar Falls and Waterloo was called Josh Higgins Parkway, named for a fictional radio character that was quite popular at the time. When the parkway was officially dedicated in 1940, 175 acres had been acquired. At an elaborate ceremony attended by dozens of dignitaries, Governor George A. Wilson promised that one day the parkway would connect the two cities.

Land acquisition continued, but a parkway along the river proved to be unfeasible: because the proposed route was too low and too near the river, flooding would be a recurring problem. A connecting road to Waterloo nonetheless was completed in 1953. At the time of Wyth's death in 1955, state landholdings had been enlarged to more than 400 acres, including substantial donations of land from Wyth himself. In 1956, the Iowa Conservation Commission renamed the parkway George Wyth Memorial State Park at the request of Cedar Falls civic leaders.

An interesting combination of historical forces produced this much-loved urban park. In the mid-1960s, the Metropolitan Planning Commission proposed developing a chain of lakes along the low-

JOHN PEARSON

lying river floodplain between Waterloo and Cedar Falls to meet increasing public demand for water-based recreation. At the same time, urban growth created pressure to build intercity expressways to move traffic efficiently. George Wyth Memorial State Park became the focal point to address both needs. Over the course of three decades and several controversies, fill dirt to build the expressways now known as Highway 58 and Interstate 380 was borrowed from the land along the river. The resulting borrow pits became three more lakes in the state park: George Wyth Lake opened in 1974 and was enlarged in 1989; East Lake opened in 1989 and was enlarged in 1997, when it was renamed Brinker Lake for a previous landowner; and Alice Wyth Lake, named for George's wife, opened in 1994.

As the park evolved, so too did recreational opportunities compatible with its natural setting. In addition to water-based recreation, many picnic areas, and a day-use lodge, the park has 3.5 miles of paved multiple-use trails and 10 miles of soft trails linked to a 100-mile trail network within the metropolitan area. The park also is a favorite with birders; more than two hundred species of birds have been observed here, and a bird-feeding station is located near the lodge.

DON POGGENSEE

# Green Valley State Park

Because creating artificial lakes for recreational use was an expensive proposition, innovative cost-sharing plans often determined which projects were feasible. To build what was initially known as Creston Lake, the Iowa Conservation Commission partnered with the city of Creston and the Southwestern Federated Power Cooperative. The lake, formed by impounding the headwaters of the Platte River in Union County, would also serve as a backup source of water for the city, and the power cooperative could draw water from the reservoir to operate its steam-electric generating station.

The September 1953 dedication ceremony celebrated completion of the dam and introduced the results of a naming contest sponsored by the Creston Chamber of Commerce. Out of five hundred entries, the winner was Green Valley State Park. Unfortunately, cracks in the dam quickly revealed design flaws and substandard construction materials. Park development was thus delayed until the 1960s while the Iowa Conservation Commission worked through expensive repairs. However, once camping, beach, fishing, and boating facilities were in place, the park became a popular destination. A designated waterskiing zone in the lake proved to be a special draw for boaters.

Over the years, the Iowa Conservation Commission and, later, the Iowa Department of Natural Resources have worked with local landowners and the Natural Resources Conservation Service to improve the surrounding watershed and reduce lake sedimentation. In 2009, the campground was extensively redeveloped and enlarged. Other amenities

IOWA DNR

include three camping cabins, two open picnic shelters, boat ramps, fish-cleaning stations, and a playground dedicated to Greg Haley, who served as park manager until his untimely death in 2009. A 10-mile multiple-use trail around the 390-acre lake takes visitors through 670 acres of wetland, woodland, and prairie habitats. A paved bike trail also connects the park to Creston and Southwestern Community College.

CARL KURTZ

# Heery Woods State Park

Heery Woods takes its name from John Heery, who in 1850 entered a claim for land along the Shell Rock River in Butler County. In 1935, his descendants sold 380 acres to the state for a nominal price on the condition that a state park be established here. The land, which lay on both sides of the river, included the 1850 tract and was heavily forested with native oak and hickory. Men employed through the Works Progress Administration developed the park by constructing a low-head dam in the river to deepen the water above for recreation and enhance fishing below, a dressed limestone lodge that resembles an English country cottage, trails and graveled drives winding through the woods, and picnic areas on both sides of the river. The park became so popular that an open picnic shelter was added to help accommodate family reunions, group meetings, and ceremonial events.

In 1974, the Butler County Conservation Board assumed management of the state park and immediately added a camping area. Since then, many amenities have been added. Conservation board headquarters were constructed in the park in 1976 and expanded in 1992. Heery Woods Nature Center, on the south side near the historic lodge, opened in 1989. The center features a discovery room with interpretive exhibits and offers a wide range of educational programs and field trips. Over the years, camping facilities have been modernized and expanded to accommodate tent campers, recreational vehicles, and equestrians. A third picnic shelter has been added, and large playgrounds are located on each side of the river. Boat, canoe, and kayak access is available above and below the dam.

MARLYS POPMA

In 2007, Heery family descendants donated an additional 10 acres of land west of the nature center to the state, which enabled an expansion of the soft trail system on the south side of the river. Trails on the north side include a horseback riding trail and a paved trail that connects to Rolling Prairie Trail, a 21-mile multiple-use trail that spans Butler, Bremer, and Franklin Counties.

# Honey Creek State Park |
# Honey Creek Resort State Park

Honey Creek State Park and Honey Creek Resort State Park are located on Rathbun Lake, the fourth U.S. Army Corps of Engineers flood-control project in Iowa. The lake was created by damming the Chariton River, which filled the valleys of several tributaries to produce an 11,000-acre reservoir surrounded by timbered rolling hills. Like the Red Rock and Saylorville projects, coordinated federal-state-local planning for multiple uses was an integral part of the Rathbun Lake project, which began operating in 1970. Honey Creek State Park is situated on a peninsula of land along the northeast shore where Honey Creek flows into the lake. Directly across Honey Creek Bay sits Honey Creek Resort, Iowa's only destination state park. They are part of a complex that includes six recreation areas created by the Corps of Engineers.

Honey Creek State Park opened for public use in 1968, with development of park facilities beginning in 1970. Today, park amenities include a large year-round modern campground, four pine-log camping cabins, two picnic shelters overlooking the lake, many picnic areas, a fish-cleaning station, and 5 miles of multiple-use trails, including an interpretive trail to eleven mounds associated with the Woodland period of American Indian habitation (800 BC–AD 1250).

Completion of the Red Rock and Rathbun lake projects stimulated decades of talk about creating resort-like state parks, but nothing substantive happened until 2000, when Governor Tom Vilsack formally recommended that the Iowa Department of Natural Resources and the Natural Resources

Commission begin planning for as many as eight parks. Five years of environmental and economic studies, architectural and engineering design work, and many public meetings eventually focused on Rathbun Lake as the one best location. Financing and construction took another three years. Honey Creek Resort State Park opened in September 2008. The complex includes a LEED-certified, 105-room lodge with a restaurant and conference center, 28 luxury cottages, campsites for recreational vehicles, an indoor waterpark and a seasonal lake aquapark, a beach, an eighteen-hole golf course, and miles of multiple-use trails—all overlooking Rathbun Lake.

In addition to managing the 828-acre park and 850-acre resort, the Iowa Department of Natural Resources also manages the 15,888-acre Rathbun Wildlife Management Area surrounding the lake and the Rathbun Fish Hatchery and Fisheries Research Station below the dam. A visitor center is located at the fish hatchery.

# Iowa Great Lakes Region

**Elinor Bedell State Park, Emerson Bay State Recreation Area, Gull Point State Park, Lower Gar State Recreation Area, Marble Beach State Recreation Area, Mini-Wakan State Park, Pikes Point State Park, Pillsbury Point State Park, Templar State Recreation Area, Trappers Bay State Park**

The cluster of natural lakes in Dickinson County, often called the Iowa Great Lakes, formed between 14,000 and 12,000 years ago during various phases of melting from the Des Moines Lobe glacier. Some of the lakes, known as kettle lakes, mark the melting of massive stranded blocks of glacial ice. Others formed along meltwater routes established under the melting ice or along its margins. Spirit Lake, the largest at nearly 5,700 acres, is also the largest natural lake in Iowa. West Lake Okoboji, the second-largest natural lake, is also the deepest, with a maximum depth of about 135 feet. Altogether, the lakes have more than 70 miles of shoreline.

MINI-WAKAN STATE PARK
DON POGGENSEE

Archaeological evidence shows that as the glacier receded, prehistoric peoples began to occupy the region. Many Oneota sites have been identified in northwest Iowa, especially along the Little Sioux River drainage from the Iowa Great Lakes to the Missouri River. Oneota refers to corn farmers from the Late Prehistoric period (AD 1250–1700) who lived in large villages throughout Iowa and the Upper Midwest. In the nineteenth century, their descendant tribes, which included the Otoe and Ioway, were gradually pushed out of northwest Iowa by federal treaties and encroaching Euro-American settlers. The Dakota were the last to leave.

There were many encounters between the Dakota and the settlers, some of them peaceful, some of them destructive. In 1857, in an outbreak of violence known as the Spirit Lake Massacre, at least thirty settlers lost their lives and four women were taken hostage. This event slowed settlement, but only temporarily. Scarcely twenty-five years later, in the mid-1880s, summer cottages and recreation spots began popping up beside the lakes. By the early 1890s, investors from as far away as Des Moines were in the market, and the lakes quickly became Iowa's foremost "pleasuring ground." Thus, when Iowa's state park system was being established, recreational development was quite advanced here.

Still, during the 1930s heyday of state park development, the state acquired land for five state parks. The first acquisition, Pillsbury Point on West

99

Lake Okoboji, was once owned by Rowland Gardner, whose daughter Abigail survived the 1857 conflict; the historic Abbie Gardner Sharp Cabin is located nearby. In the 1860s, Reverend Samuel Pillsbury owned the point, hence the park name. In 1928, heirs of a later owner donated 6 acres of the point to the state. Sites for Gull Point State Park (West Lake Okoboji), Mini-Wakan State Park (Spirit Lake), Pikes Point State Park (West Lake Okoboji), and Trappers Bay State Park (Silver Lake) were purchased, usually with community assistance.

The first five parks were developed between 1933 and 1935, primarily by Civilian Conservation Corps workers. At Gull Point, CCC crews built a large stone-and-timber lodge overlooking the lake, a stone-and-timber boathouse with a hexagonal tower, a park residence with service buildings, and entrance portals. Mini-Wakan, the Sioux name for Spirit Lake, was developed with a stone-and-timber shelter house and a combination boat-bathhouse. CCC crews also built a park road around Spirit Lake and planted three tree nurseries. At Pikes Point, crews built a stone-and-timber picnic shelter at the base of a slope and a long flight of stone steps descending the hillside. The linear park that runs along the shore of Pillsbury Point was developed with a walkway, five stone benches, and two flights of steps to the water. At Trappers Bay, CCC crews built a stone-and-timber picnic shelter; in 1941, workers hired through the National Youth Administration built an enclosed shelter house. The CCC-built structures are listed on the National Register of Historic Places, and many of them have been carefully renovated.

Between 1942 and 1987, the state acquired several spots now classified as state recreation areas. In 1942, the Iowa Conservation Commission purchased a mile and a half of wooded shoreline on the west bank of Spirit Lake. The tract was named Marble Beach for William and Margaret Marble, victims of the violence of 1857; in 1958, it was developed as a tent-and-trailer campground. Today, Marble Beach is the largest campground in the Iowa Great Lakes region, with modern and nonmodern campsites, boat ramps, and a paved trail that connects to other recreational trails.

By the early 1960s, the Iowa Conservation Commission also had a campground at Gull Point State Park as well as Emerson Bay on West Lake Okoboji. At Emerson Bay, the state purchased an adjacent 5-acre parcel in 1978 and later developed it as a day-use area with a shelter house and an observation tower overlooking the lake. In 1971, the ICC purchased 25 acres on the west side of Lower Gar Lake, including 2,000 feet of shoreline access. This area was developed primarily for shoreline fishing, although it also has a boat ramp and a picnic area. In 1987, the Iowa Department of Natural Resources purchased Templar Park, situated on a small bay on the west side of Spirit Lake. The Knights Templar, a fraternal organization, had established a meeting ground here in 1890 and later built a large resort. The original entrance arch remains, but the site is now a picnic area with a shelter and two gazebos; a boat launch is located in the bay.

The newest state park in the lakes region began as a gift from Berkley and Elinor Bedell, who in 1998 donated 80 acres on the shore of East Okoboji

Lake. Berkley represented northwest Iowa in the U.S. Congress from 1975 to 1987. In 2001, the park was dedicated as Elinor Bedell State Park, and a portion was developed with a small modern campground, a hike-in/canoe-in youth group campground, a day-use shelter overlooking the lake, and a playground specifically for young children. An extensive system of universally accessible trails takes visitors through prairie, wetland, and savanna landscapes.

In addition to these developed state parks and recreation areas, there are several more state-owned access points for fishing and boat launching. The Iowa Department of Natural Resources also manages several thousand acres of wildlife areas in the vast watershed surrounding the lakes. The Okoboji Protective Association, Spirit Lake Protective Association, East Okoboji Lake Improvement Corporation, Iowa Lakeside Laboratory, and other member organizations of the Iowa Great Lakes Association also promote lake and watershed stewardship.

# Kearny State Park

Stephen W. Kearny (sometimes spelled Kearney), who is better known for his military command of U.S. forces in the Mexican-American War, also played a role in westward expansion. In 1820, he was with the first military expedition to explore the territory between Fort Atkinson, Nebraska, and Fort Snelling, Minnesota. In 1834, he became commander of Fort Des Moines, in what is now Montrose, Iowa, and the next year he led the horse-mounted soldiers of the First Dragoon Regiment on a twelve-week expedition through central Iowa and southern Minnesota. During both expeditions, his company camped near the present site of Emmetsburg on the shores of what is now called Five Island Lake. Nearly a century later, in 1940, the state purchased parkland in the approximate location of this encampment. The State Historical Society of Iowa asked that it be named after Kearny "as a memorial to a distinguished American officer of dragoons who twice crossed Iowa."

The 40-acre park provides public access to Five Island Lake, once known as Medium Lake, a shallow natural lake of nearly a thousand acres. Repeated dredging to enhance its use for water recreation has revealed submerged archaeological deposits. After a dredge operator reported the presence of artifacts and fossilized bones in lake sediment, archaeologists studied multiple spoil sites. The dredged collections show that American Indian peoples hunted, trapped, and fished in and around the lake for more than 8,000 years.

Since 1960, the city of Emmetsburg has managed the park under an agreement with the Iowa Department of Natural Resources. Park facilities

JOHN PEARSON

include modern and nonmodern camping sites, a beachside picnic and playground area, boat launches, and a universally accessible fishing pier.

WARREN TERPSTRA

# Lacey-Keosauqua State Park

Lacey-Keosauqua was one of two state parks dedicated in 1920, the other being Backbone. It is named for John F. Lacey—Civil War veteran, attorney, and U.S. congressman from Iowa from 1888 to 1890 and 1892 to 1906—who was a strong advocate for federal conservation laws to protect natural resources and antiquities on public lands. There is considerable debate about the origin and meaning of the name Keosauqua, with no clear consensus. The park lies along the outside curve of a great bend in the river as it courses through Van Buren County. Outcrops of Mississippian age limestone and sandstone occur in the bend and can be seen from Ely Ford, where Mormons crossed the river during their great trek westward in the 1840s.

The land for Lacey-Keosauqua was purchased with a mix of public and private funds, which set the tone for park development. Groups and individuals who had worked hard to pass the 1917 State Park Act stressed the law's conservation mandate. Local citizens who had contributed several thousand dollars to buy the land wanted the park developed for recreation. Louis Pammel, first chair of the Iowa State Board of Conservation, resolved the disagreement by hiring a landscape architect to create a park master plan that could accomplish both ends. By the late 1920s, the park had campgrounds, trails, picnic areas, a lodge, and a nine-hole golf course (no longer present). It also preserved sacred Native American burial mounds, historic sites, and wooded areas for the study of native plants and animals.

Recreational amenities drew increasing numbers of park visitors. During the Great Depression, the state took advantage of federal relief funds to fully develop

JOSEPH STANSKI

the park. Workers with the Civilian Conservation Corps, the Works Progress Administration, and other New Deal programs enlarged the lodge, turned a former millpond into a 30-acre lake, and built dozens of stone-and-timber buildings and other structures, which are listed on the National Register of Historic Places. The lake and beach, with nearby cabins and a campground, are still an attractive family destination. Recently, the Iowa Department of Natural Resources, in collaboration with the Friends of Lacey-Keosauqua State Park, converted an old stone entrance station near the lodge into a mini-interpretive center and erected a life-size bronze statue of a CCC worker, called Iron Mike.

The CCC built dams to control soil erosion and established a nursery to provide stock for park landscaping and reforestation. Lacey-Keosauqua's 1,653 acres continue to support numerous outdoor activities as well as protect several plant, animal, and aquatic species. The park is part of a nearly 8,000-acre conservation landscape that includes the Keosauqua Unit of Shimek State Forest, Lake Sugema Wildlife Management Area, and Lake Sugema County Park.

105

JIM SCHEFFLER

# Lake Ahquabi State Park

Lake Ahquabi State Park was one of many artificial lake parks developed in the 1950s to carry out recommendations in the Iowa Twenty-five Year Conservation Plan. Noted political cartoonist and conservationist Jay N. "Ding" Darling reportedly selected the site, located in Warren County about 25 miles south of Des Moines. In 1934, the city of Indianola purchased the site—560 acres of eroded farmland—and donated it to the state. A resident of Norwalk won a contest to name the new state park, which was dedicated in 1936. At the time, the name Ahquabi was said to be an Amerindian word meaning "resting place," although a Meskwaki tribal member informed the press that it did not. Language scholars have since noted that Ahquabi does not closely match the vocabularies of any Native American tribe historically associated with Iowa. Still, the supposed meaning aptly describes the park and has been repeated so often that it is accepted at face value.

The goal of park development was to create a "scenic lake and park enhanced by the natural rolling woodlands of southern Iowa." Between 1934 and 1937, Civilian Conservation Corps workers planted trees and constructed a 140-acre lake along with roads, hiking trails, picnic areas, a group camping area, and several rustic stone structures, including a picnic shelter, a bathhouse, a lodge, and three fountains. Even while park features and facilities were under construction, the park was heavily used, which is not surprising given its proximity to the state capital.

As early as 1939, siltation became a noticeable problem, which the Iowa Conservation Commission addressed by acquiring more land around the lake and

JOHN PEARSON

working with landowners to control soil erosion. In the post–World War II era, as larger lakes and multiple-use flood-control reservoirs gradually appeared in central Iowa, Lake Ahquabi remained a favorite. Today, the park covers 770 acres, including the 115-acre lake. Visitors enjoy 7 miles of multiple-use trails, a no-wake lake that is popular with paddlers, a universally accessible fishing pier, a modern campground, and restored historic stone-and-timber park buildings.

107

# Lake Anita State Park

Lake Anita is one of eight new lake parks created during the second wave of artificial lake projects authorized by the legislature in 1947 and undertaken in the 1950s and 1960s. Land acquisition for Lake Anita began in 1961, but construction of the dam was delayed until 1963. The resulting lake, which impounds the waters of Turkey Creek watershed, has an irregular shoreline that traces the contours of three valleys in the rolling terrain of the older glacial plains across southern Iowa. A park service building and residence were constructed in 1965. Park development was completed in 1968 with the construction of beach facilities, a bathhouse, and eight picnic shelters. Named for the nearby town of Anita, the park was dedicated in 1969.

Lake Anita quickly became a popular destination for fishing, swimming, picnicking, and camping and remains so today. In 2013 and 2014, the Iowa Department of Natural Resources conducted a major restoration project to reduce siltation and control aquatic vegetation. This and the acquisition of the 112-acre Lake Anita Wildlife Management Area, adjacent to the park on the east side, have helped maintain healthy fisheries and water quality for outdoor recreation.

The park now covers 1,062 acres, including the lake. Amenities include ample modern camping facilities, a playground, two boat ramps for access to the no-wake lake, and several picnic areas overlooking the lake. A 4-mile paved trail that connects the town of Anita with all the park facilities winds around the lake and through diverse habitats, including restored prairie. A short self-guided trail

MARLYS POPMA

provides information about trees and shrubs found in southwest Iowa. Seasonal hunting is permitted in the wildlife management area.

DON POGGENSEE

# Lake Cornelia State Park

Lake Cornelia is one of several small natural lakes in Wright County that formed along a hummocky moraine left by the Des Moines Lobe glacier between 15,000 and 12,000 years ago. Older maps sometimes call this body of water Little Wall Lake, but the name Lake Cornelia was in use as early as 1875. According to early accounts, the name honors Cornelia Eastman Hancock (1838–1921) of the nearby town of Clarion, one of the first teachers in the county. During the late nineteenth century, a rail stop and commercial area called Cornelia sprang up on the east shore. Private landowners began to erect bathhouses, boat liveries, and other concessions and subdivide land for summer cottages.

By 1915, according to one observer, the lake was "nothing but a rectangular marsh, covering about a half-section, crowded from side to side with rank aquatic vegetation." But it was also an established recreation area associated with Clarion, which may have saved it from being drained for farmland, as happened to many of Iowa's shallow glacial lakes. During the 1950s, Clarion civic leaders began to petition the Iowa Conservation Commission for action, asking why the state was "building lakes and damming streams to make others, but still overlooks a good sized 'puddle' already present, now in need of assistance."

The result, eventually, was Lake Cornelia State Park. In 1941, the legislature appropriated funds to dredge the lake and purchase adjacent land for park purposes. Dredging operations began in 1942, but wartime budget cuts forced the Iowa Conservation Commission to suspend work. The dredging was not finished until 1948, and the ICC never got around to improving the park beyond adding changing

MARLYS POPMA

booths for swimmers. In 1957, the Clarion Junior Chamber of Commerce entered into an agreement with the ICC to develop and maintain a 55-acre park on the northwest shore of the lake. That same year, the Lake Cornelia Improvement Association was formed to address the health of the lake as a whole. In 1964, park management was transferred to the Wright County Conservation Board. In 1975, the board purchased land north of the state-owned land, and the enlarged park was finally developed for recreation. Today, the 122-acre park offers visitors open and enclosed shelters, a boat marina and fishing jetty, modern camping facilities, playfields, a beach, and a walking trail.

# Lake Darling State Park

It is hard to overstate Lake Darling's significance in the Iowa state park system. The name honors Pulitzer Prize–winning cartoonist Jay N. "Ding" Darling (1876–1962) of the *Des Moines Register*, who for more than forty years used his barbed wit and ferocious pen to expose political chicanery, critique "nature lovers" and thoughtless hunters, and demand better treatment of our lands and waters. Darling, an avid outdoorsman and outspoken conservationist, was also the visionary behind the 1933 Iowa Twenty-five Year Conservation Plan. In adopting this comprehensive plan, the legislature brought the management of all state lands and waters under one agency—the Iowa Conservation Commission—in order to carry out myriad interrelated goals. One of these goals was to create artificial lakes in southern Iowa to complement the state's existing natural lakes, primarily located in the northern half, so that all Iowans had access to a lake for fishing and water recreation.

Not only was Darling alive when Lake Darling State Park was dedicated on September 17, 1950—which in itself speaks to his extraordinary influence—but he participated in the ceremony by setting the gate to begin filling the impoundment on Honey Creek, a tributary of the Skunk River in Washington County. The resulting lake sits nestled amid numerous sloping hillsides that are typical of the older, well-drained glacial deposits across most of southern Iowa. During the 1950s, the park was developed with picnic areas, campgrounds, a beach house, boat ramps, and trails. However, a very large watershed drains into the lake, and by 2000 sedimentation had reduced its size from 302 to 267 acres, and water quality was poor. Moreover, park facilities were dilapidated.

The park that visitors find today is the result of a major undertaking that essentially re-created the lake and its surroundings. Between 2000 and September 17, 2014, when the park was rededicated, the lake was drained and reengineered, more than 300,000 cubic feet of silt were removed, and existing facilities were replaced and augmented with new ones. At the same time, the Iowa Department of Natural Resources and the Natural Resources Conservation Service worked with landowners to control erosion and runoff from the 12,500-acre watershed. What makes this undertaking more significant is the level of cooperation and funding assistance that came from landowners, private organizations, and community stakeholders, including the Friends of Lake Darling State Park, the Izaak Walton League, and the Washington County Riverboat Foundation.

The park now covers 1,387 acres, including the lake. Visitors enjoy an all-season lodge that covers 4,000 square feet, a universally accessible fishing trail, five seasonal camping cabins, six year-round universally accessible family cabins, and the half-mile universally accessible Ding Darling Interpretive Pathway.

# Lake Keomah State Park

Although the name Keomah has the melodic sound of an Amerindian word, it is a portmanteau created from two southeastern Iowa county names: Keokuk and Mahaska, which in turn are the names of Native American leaders. Many residents from both counties contributed funds to purchase land along a tributary of the South Skunk River where water could be impounded in the steeply rolling landscape. As a mark of widespread enthusiasm for a lake park, retail stores in the nearby city of Oskaloosa closed for two hours on Tuesday, October 8, 1933, so that townspeople could attend the groundbreaking ceremony for construction of the dam. One stipulation of local support was the reservation of shorefront land for private development, which became Lake Keomah Village.

Between 1933 and 1937, the park was developed with federal assistance primarily through the Civilian Conservation Corps but also through the Civil Works Administration and the National Youth Administration. CCC crews created the lake, planted trees, and constructed roads and trails as well as a stone boat-bathhouse with a distinctive octagonal check-in room and a large stone lodge. In July 2003, the 566-acre park was rededicated following major renovations to the historic buildings. In addition to the day-use lodge and boat-bathhouse, these include a group camp building, the latter being located in a formal group campground with a separate access road. Visitors enjoy multiple picnic areas, a quiet no-wake lake, a modern campground separate from the group camping area, a universally accessible fishing jetty, and a shoreline trail that travels through a variety of habitats as well as Lake Keomah Village.

MARLYS POPMA

# Lake Macbride State Park

Lake Macbride is a state park in two acts. For many years, a scenic wooded area along Mill Creek in Johnson County had been of interest as a park location. Fieldwork for the Iowa Twenty-five Year Conservation Plan, which involved many knowledgeable people throughout the state, turned that interest into the first act. In 1933, the Iowa City Chamber of Commerce organized a local effort to purchase 800 acres of land to create an artificial lake park by damming the waters of Mill Creek as well as Jordan Creek just before they joined the Iowa River. The land purchase was financed by selling lots for cottage sites on a 75-acre peninsula that would jut into the resulting lake. The state provided engineering and design work for the project, which took more than three years to complete. Between late 1933 and 1937, Civilian Conservation Corps crews provided most of the labor to clear land, create erosion-control features, plant trees, quarry rock, build the dam, and then develop the park.

As work was underway, the park was turned over to the state, cost-free, and dedicated as Lake Macbride State Park on May 30, 1934. The name honors Thomas H. Macbride (1848–1934), professor of botany at the University of Iowa, president of the university from 1914 to 1916, a passionate conservationist, and one of the earliest advocates for county and state parks. Upon his death, his colleague Bohumil Shimek eulogized him as the person who, in the 1890s, initiated "the campaign which resulted in our present state-park system" by urging the Iowa Academy of Science to advocate for a statewide system of rural parks and take the lead in watershed protection as well as forest conservation.

The park's second act began in the early 1940s, when the U.S. Army Corps of Engineers proposed to build a flood-control dam on the Iowa River north of Iowa City. Local citizens as well as the Iowa Conservation Commission challenged the project because it would ruin Lake Macbride. Federal and state agencies eventually negotiated an agreement whereby the Corps of Engineers would acquire more land and raise the lake dam high enough to create a barrier between Lake Macbride and the new reservoir, which became known as Coralville Lake. The work, completed in 1957, enlarged Lake Macbride from about 140 acres to more than 900 acres. The peninsula, known as Cottage Reserve, was reduced in size, but the park as a whole was increased to nearly 2,200 acres, making it one of the larger state parks in Iowa.

Today, the park is part of a huge outdoor recreation complex that includes Coralville Lake and recreation areas, the University of Iowa–managed Macbride Nature Recreation Area, and Hawkeye Wildlife Management Area. Nonetheless, it remains one of Iowa's most serene state parks, with fishing and no-wake boating on the lake, 7 miles of shoreline and wooded hiking trails, modern and nonmodern campgrounds, and several picnic areas. A 5-mile multiple-use trail connects the park to nearby Solon, with further connections to Cedar Rapids via the Hoover Nature Trail and Cedar Falls via the Cedar Valley Nature Trail.

# Lake Manawa State Park

"Manawa" is said to be a Native American word meaning "peace and comfort," but language scholars have determined that it most closely resembles the Ojibwa word "minawa," which means "again, more, anew." Whatever its derivation, early residents bestowed the name after the flood of 1881 rechanneled the Missouri River and left this large oxbow lake on the Iowa side.

Although the lake, as a body of water formed by nature, was sovereign territory under Iowa state law, the land around it was privately owned and developed. Steamboats and then electric streetcars beckoned urban dwellers to what became known as the Coney Island of the Midwest, complete with a bathing resort at Manhattan Beach. Other attractions included toboggan slides into the lake, an amusement park featuring a roller coaster and skating rink, a boardwalk pavilion with eating places, and a vaudeville hall. The Kursaal, a two-story dancehall and restaurant, perched over the water, and a casino owned by the notorious Ben Marks sat nearby. But the lake's entertainment heyday was relatively short-lived. A series of tragic accidents, a devastating tornado in 1913, and the prohibition of alcohol all led to decreasing crowds. After fire destroyed the pavilion in 1926, the resort closed a year later.

The Great Depression opened the way for developing Lake Manawa as a state park, which the Iowa Conservation Commission had identified as a desirable location as early as 1919. During the 1950s, the lake was dredged to deepen the northeast portion, and the spoil was deposited to create the peninsula now used for picnicking, shoreline fishing, and boat

JIM SCHEFFLER

launching. Since then, repeated dredging has continued to deepen the lake, and a pump helps maintain the water level by drawing water from Mosquito Creek. Between 1966 and 1986, picnic and day-use facilities were expanded and a supervised beach facility was built at a new location. Today the park, including the lake, covers more than 1,500 acres. The local community has also been involved in park improvements, Dream Playground being the most notable project. Designed from ideas submitted by elementary school children and constructed with volunteer labor, the playground opened in 1993. In 2015, a second community-based steering committee launched a repeat effort to update and expand this popular playground, and the work was completed in 2018.

# Lake Odessa Campground

Lake Odessa in Louisa County is a large complex of backwaters and islands along the floodplain west of the Mississippi River's main channel. The broad alluvial plain here was formed by past migrations of the Mississippi, rearranging sediments brought by earlier volumes of glacial meltwaters, especially during waning of the Wisconsin age ice sheet from the Upper Midwest 12,000 years ago.

It is unclear how Lake Odessa acquired its name, but in 1861 a town named Odessa was platted on the northwest edge of the lake, and riverboats are said to have tied up at a landing there. The town did not survive, and in 1914 the state ordered the lake drained. This did not happen right away, and in 1919, Louis Pammel and E. R. Harlan, chair and secretary of the Iowa State Board of Conservation, inspected Lake Odessa and nearby Lake Meyerholz and reportedly were "favorably impressed with these locations as state parks."

However, by late 1920, Lake Odessa, then described as 500 acres in size, and several other small lakes had been drained. A system of canals and pumping stations turned the "Muscatine slough" into farmable bottomland. Then, between 1930 and 1940, the U.S. Army Corps of Engineers' nine-foot channel project along the Upper Mississippi River brought dramatic new changes. Seepage from the pool above Lock and Dam No. 17, adjacent to the old slough, reflooded the bottomland and created a much-larger Lake Odessa.

In the mid-1940s, the Corps of Engineers turned management of the restored and expanded wetlands over to the U.S. Fish and Wildlife Service, and the

JIM SCHEFFLER

Iowa Conservation Commission then entered into an initial agreement with the Fish and Wildlife Service to manage the Lake Odessa area for waterfowl hunting and fishing. In 1949, the Louisa County Chapter of the Izaak Walton League raised funds for the Iowa Conservation Commission to purchase 5 acres at Shaefer's Point for public access on the west side of the lake. The ICC constructed a road from County Road X61 to the access area and progressively developed it into a campground. It remains a quiet, nonmodern campground with a limited number of sites.

Since the mid-1950s, management of the nearly 6,500-acre Odessa Wildlife Complex has been split between the Iowa Department of Natural Resources, which manages the 4,139-acre Odessa Wildlife Management Area, and the U.S. Fish and Wildlife Service, which manages the Port Louisa National Wildlife Refuge to the north.

BRIAN GIBBS

# Lake of Three Fires State Park

Lake of Three Fires memorializes the Prairie and Forest bands of the Potawatomi, who settled in southwest Iowa for a time in the mid-nineteenth century as multiple federal treaties gradually forced them south and west onto a reservation in Kansas. The name Potawatomi is derived from an Ojibwe word that means "people of the place of fire" or variants thereof. Three Fires refers to a long-standing confederacy of the Ojibwe, Ottawa, and Potawatomi, sometimes known as the Council of Three Fires.

One of many artificial lake parks developed in the 1930s, Lake of Three Fires came about after local residents purchased 375 acres of steeply rolling woodland in Taylor County and donated them to the state in 1935 for a park. The focal point was to be a recreational lake, also to serve as an auxiliary water source for the city of Bedford. Crews hired through the Works Progress Administration built a dam to impound a tributary of the East Fork of the One Hundred and Two River. Civilian Conservation Corps workers constructed a bathhouse, swimming beach, picnic area, and fish-rearing ponds.

In 1955, the Bedford Saddle Club formed to help develop riding trails and an equestrian campground on the east side of the park. Between 1997 and 2005, the 85-acre lake was extensively reengineered to reduce sedimentation, improve water quality, and restore fisheries. Wildlife management areas located northwest and south of the park, which now totals 691 acres, provide additional watershed protection as well as public hunting in season. Park amenities include two modern campgrounds, six rental cabins, picnic shelters, 8 miles of multiple-use trails, and

IOWA DNR

boat ramps. The beachside bathhouse has been renovated into a seasonal lodge for day use.

# Lake Wapello State Park

Lake Wapello was the first of many artificial lakes constructed in the 1930s to carry out a favored recommendation of the Iowa Twenty-five Year Conservation Plan: create more lake parks in areas of the state where there were few so that all Iowans were within easy driving distance of a recreation spot. The park's name honors the Meskwaki chief who helped negotiate six land cession treaties between 1822 and 1837. Wapello, however, is best remembered for his impassioned 1841 speech resisting further removal. The reprieve proved to be temporary. Wapello died on March 15, 1842, and the final Meskwaki land cession was formalized later that year. He was buried at Agency, Iowa, approximately 30 miles northeast of the park. His interment site is now Chief Wapello's Memorial Park, which is listed on the National Register of Historic Places.

The lake project got underway in late 1932 after the state acquired a tract of steeply rolling land in western Davis County where the waters of Pee Dee Creek could be impounded. Local support was overwhelming. Residents from the surrounding area contributed more than $10,000 as well as volunteer labor. By February 1, 1933, 1,050 days of labor had been donated to remove timber and fences within the waterline. After the Civilian Conservation Corps was up and running, CCC crews took over, completing the dam and erosion-control structures before the end of the year. CCC workers also planted tens of thousands of trees and built roads, trails, fish-rearing ponds, and an elegant stone-and-timber combination boat-bathhouse, which is now a day-use rental lodge. Boat rentals are offered on the weekends by the Friends of Lake Wapello.

IOWA DNR

Lake Wapello State Park, now 1,150 acres in size, including the lake, is still a quiet refuge. It offers visitors a modern campground, a complex of thirteen cedar-sided cabins, originally built as a "fisherman's village," and several picnic areas. The no-wake lake was extensively renovated in the early 1990s and again in 2009. It has beach and fishing facilities, including universally accessible fishing piers, and is surrounded by a 7-mile shoreline trail.

# Ledges State Park

Ledges is one of Iowa's best-loved parks. Long before the State Park Act passed in 1917, sightseers and natural scientists were making day trips to the picturesque sandstone ledges that tower above Pea's Creek, named for John Pea, one of the earliest settlers in Boone County. The steep walls of Pea's Creek Canyon were carved 14,000 to 12,000 years ago by glacial meltwater cutting through massive outcrops of Pennsylvanian age sandstone. Ledges was high on the list of proposed state park sites. After local residents donated funds to help purchase the initial 644 acres, the state purchased additional acreage in the 1930s and 1940s.

During the 1920s, the Iowa State Board of Conservation improved the park with new roads, picnic and camp sites, footbridges, and three buildings: a "commissary," a "greeting cabin," and a caretaker's residence, all built of rough-log construction. Carl Fritz Henning, caretaker from 1921 to 1941, fenced an enclosure for deer and built dens to hold native fur-bearing animals, an early version of today's nature centers, which added to the park's popularity. During the 1930s, Civilian Conservation Corps crews added hiking trails, large parking areas, additional picnic grounds, a combined shelter-concession building, a new caretaker's residence, and rental cabins. After Henning died in 1941, the Iowa Conservation Commission decided to close the zoo, although some live-animal exhibits remained until 1981.

Ledges is also the state park that Iowans have fought the hardest to preserve. Shortly after the park was established, a power company requested permission to overflow about 150 acres as part of a proposed series of hydroelectric dams on the Des Moines River. Local sentiments were divided, but the Board of Conservation was not. The board managed to thwart this proposal, but the Iowa Conservation Commission later faced a much tougher challenge from the U.S. Army Corps of Engineers when flood control became a major public concern in the 1950s.

The Saylorville dam project on the Des Moines River, as originally proposed in 1959, would have subjected Pea's Creek Canyon to increased flooding, and the ICC went on record as opposed. World War II and then lack of funding held the project up until the early 1970s. By then, the environmental movement was gaining momentum, and several environmental groups joined the Iowa Citizens' Alliance to Save Ledges State Park. After several years of wrangling— in public hearings, in court, and in the press—the Corps of Engineers and the Conservation Commission settled on a solution that would reduce the incidence and duration of flooding. Even so, repeated flooding eventually led the Iowa Department of Natural Resources, in 1998, to dismantle the 1930s shelter-concession building, stone by stone, and move it to higher ground. After restoration, the building was dedicated as the Carl Fritz Henning Shelter.

Ledges is still one of Iowa's signature state parks. Its varied landscape holds wooded slopes, native and restored prairies, streams, bottomlands, and wetlands, which provide habitat for an astounding 599 species of native vascular plants. Several of the historic stone structures remain. Modern camping facilities are situated near the east entrance, and there are many wonders to discover along the 4.5 miles of carefully restored hiking trails that run through this scenic 1,115-acre park.

# Lewis and Clark State Park

In May of 1804, Meriwether Lewis, secretary to President Thomas Jefferson, and Captain William Clark, U.S. Army, set out from St. Louis with twenty-six men, navigating the Missouri River in a keelboat. Known as the Corps of Discovery, their goal was to find "the most direct and practicable water communication across the continent, for the purposes of commerce." By August, the expedition had made its way up the river as far as present-day Iowa. According to the journals of Clark and others, on August 10 the party passed a spot in the river called Coupée à Jacques (Jacques' Cut), a place where the meandering river had cut a more direct channel, in the process forming an oxbow believed to be the body of water now known as Blue Lake.

In 1919, the Iowa State Board of Conservation identified Blue Lake as a potential site for a state park. Local residents had long used the lake and surrounding area for fishing, hunting, and picnicking, and in the early 1920s, the Onawa Country Club laid out a golf course near the lake. The golf course was relocated in 1924, when the state exchanged farmable land in the old lakebed for parkland adjacent to the lake. It was named Lewis and Clark to memorialize the two men who led the storied expedition to the Pacific Northwest. In 1928 the Onawa Community Club and American Legion Post raised money to construct a bathhouse for swimmers. During the 1930s, the Board of Conservation further improved the park with roads, trails, and a rustic lodge.

Everything changed with the historic Missouri River Flood of 1952, which deposited up to 5 feet of silt in parts of the lake, drastically altering fishing

and boating conditions. After years of study and funding delays, a portion of the lake was dredged in 1979 and 1980. The dredged section produced a smaller lake for boating, and the undredged area was left as a marsh, which is now a wildlife management area surrounding the 250-acre lake and 176-acre park. As at Lake Manawa, a pumping system helps maintain the water level.

The 1930s lodge still stands, joined in 2012 by a modern educational and interpretive center that is now one of the park's two focal points. The other is a replica of the keelboat, *Best Friend*, used by the Corps of Discovery. In 1986 and 1987, a group of volunteers constructed a historically accurate version, and visitors can schedule a ride in a working keelboat. The park displays replicas of all six of the expedition's boats.

KEN FORMANEK

# Maquoketa Caves State Park

The awe-inspiring Natural Bridge arching over Raccoon Creek at Maquoketa Caves State Park is an icon of Iowa geology. This unusual feature was once part of a cave roof in a network of thirteen dolomite caves and collapsed sinkholes along a wooded ravine near the Maquoketa River in Jackson County. Geologist James Lees called the caves one of Iowa's unique regions. They are the best place in Iowa to observe the karst features characteristic of caves, sinkholes, and underground drainage through Silurian age dolomite.

The easy accessibility of these usually subterranean features has attracted humans for millennia. In the nineteenth century, locals gave individual caves and formations descriptive names such as Pulpit, Shinbone, and Dancehall. The name Dancehall suggests that cave exploring led to other popular group activities, and historic photographs show that a dance pavilion once stood near Natural Bridge. Easy accessibility also prompted the Iowa State Board of Conservation to acquire this exceptionally scenic, scientific, and educational resource as a state park.

Park development did not begin until the early 1950s, when the Board of Conservation erected a staff residence, designed by landscape architect John R. Fitzsimmons. During the Great Depression, Civilian Conservation Corps and Works Progress Administration crews constructed a lodge and concession building, three toadstool-shaped stone-and-timber picnic shelters, a distinctive picnic circle, and park entrance portals; these are listed on the National Register of Historic Places. They also built a combination retaining wall and concrete walkway

in Dancehall Cave. This marked the beginning of an often challenging effort to protect the thirteen caves and other fragile geological formations while allowing visitors, who came in increasing numbers each year, to continue to enjoy them.

Over the decades, the state has acquired surrounding land to buffer the caves and provide space for camping facilities and additional trails; the park now covers 323 acres. Three youth camps accommodate the unusually large number of young people who come to experience the caves. An extensive system of stairs and boardwalks makes it easier for visitors of all ages to explore the caves. The park's rugged terrain is heavily forested with a mixture of residual old-growth stands dominated by white oak, red oak, and sugar maple; second-growth stands dominated by elm, ash, and walnut; and a pine plantation near the campground.

Many recorded archaeological sites provide evidence that Native American peoples used the caves and rock shelters in this area for more than 6,000 years before pioneer settlement. In 1988, the state acquired the Sagers Museum, a limestone block building near the park entrance, and converted it into a visitor center. The center interprets the geological history of the region and displays a portion of Paul and Fay Sagers' collection of artifacts excavated from rock shelters along the Maquoketa River. Most of the Sagers' collection was donated to the University of Iowa, where researchers use it to understand the past.

# Margo Frankel Woods State Park

Margo Frankel Woods honors Margo Kohn Frankel of Des Moines, who was appointed to the Iowa State Board of Conservation in 1927 and to its successor, the Iowa Conservation Commission, in 1935. During her tenure, from 1927 to 1935, she chaired both bodies. She also served on the board of the National Conference on State Parks, and in 1933 she received an award from the American Scenic and Historic Preservation Society for her contributions to Iowa's state park system.

In 1946, a group known as the Greater Des Moines Committee raised funds to purchase a 102-acre wooded tract in Saylor Township and donated it to the state for a park. Long known as Saylor Woods, the area initially was declared a refuge. After Frankel died in 1948, her husband, Henry, donated additional land; the name was changed to Margo Frankel Woods; and the refuge was reclassified as a state park.

Since its creation, the park has functioned more as a community park. In 1951, the Ding Darling Chapter of the Izaak Walton League created a nature trail. In the early 1960s, a paved nature trail was added to accommodate children attending Easterseals Iowa Camp Sunnyside, which was constructed adjacent to the park. The Saylorville Jaycees donated playground equipment in 1981. In 1992, after years of discussion, Saylor Township trustees assumed management of the 140-acre park under an agreement with the Iowa Department of Natural Resources. The trustees, with considerable volunteer labor, improved the playground and constructed new shelter houses to replace those built in the 1970s. Boy Scouts from Urbandale built steps to help visitors negotiate hillside nature trails.

# Mines of Spain State Recreation Area | Catfish Creek State Preserve

Mines are places where the intersection of geologic time and human history is especially obvious, and so it is with Mines of Spain south of Dubuque. The immense forces of water that deepened the Mississippi River valley as glaciers melted from the Upper Midwest about 12,000 years ago not only produced scenic blufflands and an intricate inland waterway, they also exposed veins of galena, a lead-bearing mineral found within crevices and cave openings of Ordovician age dolomite rocks.

The name Mines of Spain refers to Julien Dubuque's lead mines along the Mississippi River. Dubuque, an entrepreneurial French Canadian, came to Prairie du Chien around 1785, then moved farther downriver and settled among the Meskwaki near the mouth of Catfish Creek. In 1788, he negotiated an agreement with the Meskwaki that gave him exclusive permission to work their lead mines. By then Spain had claimed most of the land west of the Mississippi, and thus Dubuque also sought a land grant from the Spanish governor of Louisiana, which he received in 1796. He called this land grant Mines of Spain. Dubuque mined lead here with the Meskwaki and built up an extensive enterprise that employed a large multiethnic workforce. Upon his death in 1810, the Meskwaki buried him on top of a bluff overlooking the river and later erected a wooden building over his grave. In 1897, the Early Settlers' Association built a limestone tower to mark his gravesite.

Lead mining here began during the prehistoric period and continued until the Fessler mine closed in 1914. The Meskwaki dug out galena and smelted it

CATFISH CREEK
PAMELA BRANDT

after they moved into the area in the early eighteenth century; when they were forcibly moved westward after the 1832 Black Hawk War, Euro-American settlers took over their mines. Before them, other groups had dug the silvery gray galena for ornamental as well as utilitarian purposes. In 1634, French explorer Jean Nicolet learned about the galena deposits on the Wisconsin side of the river from the Ho-Chunk (Winnebago), indicating that mineral extraction in the Upper Mississippi River valley was a well-established practice before historical written accounts began. More than 250 documented archaeological sites in Mines of Spain attest to continuous human occupation here for over 8,000 years. Several mound groups from the Woodland period show that by about 800 BC the area was being extensively used, and by AD 1250 settled agricultural communities were present.

In 1919, the Iowa State Board of Conservation identified Catfish Creek as a potential state park. Similarly, the 1933 Twenty-five Year Conservation Plan noted that the high bluffs overlooking the Upper Mississippi River were "the outstanding scenic asset" of northeastern Iowa and demanded their preservation. However, this storied place did not come into the system until 1980, when the Iowa Natural Heritage Foundation seized an opportunity to purchase 1,240 acres of bluffs along the river, including the mouth of Catfish Creek. The state, in turn, purchased the property from the foundation. Land acquisitions since then have enlarged state holdings to 1,439 acres. In 1991, 600 acres in the northern half were dedicated as a geological, archaeological, and historical state preserve. In 1980, the state assumed management of the E.B. Lyons Interpretive Center and grounds from the city of Dubuque on a long-term lease. Mines of Spain is also a National Historic Landmark, a Silos and Smokestacks National Heritage Area Partner Site, and a National Wildlife Federation Nature Area.

Mines of Spain is archaeologically rich and, thus, lightly developed. Picnic grounds in the northern area are located at the interpretive center, Julien Dubuque Monument, and Riprow Valley. In the southern area, Horseshoe Bluff, an old limestone quarry, contains a picnic area, an interpretive trail explaining the local geology and history, and a loop trail around a wetland with a wildlife observation deck. The extensive trail system is a component of the National Recreational Trail system. A canoe launch at Catfish Creek provides access to the 11-mile Dubuque Water Trail. Hunting is allowed in portions of the state recreation area on a seasonal basis. A good starting point for visitors is the E.B. Lyons Interpretive Center, a superior facility with an active corps of volunteers assisting the staff.

HORSESHOE BLUFF
PAMELA BRANDT

# Nine Eagles State Park

According to legend, the first white settlers in this area of Decatur County, near the Iowa-Missouri border, observed nine eagles roosting in the trees above them, and a place-name sprang to mind. One of those settlers may have been Allen Scott, said to be a folkloric rough-and-tumble sort. Sometime in the 1840s, Scott established a trading post, mill, and post office in the vicinity of what is now the state park. The post office was named Nine Eagles.

Now fast-forward some ninety years. In 1940, after obtaining an option on a tract of land, a delegation from Decatur County approached the Iowa Conservation Commission about developing it as a state park. The ICC agreed to purchase the land, then began acquiring additional parcels. A year later, in May 1941, the ICC announced that the new state park, now "under development," would be called Nine Eagles, thus immortalizing the legendary name.

The development plan hinged on the availability of Civilian Conservation Corps labor, which was abundant in the 1930s, but when the United States entered World War II in December 1941, CCC enrollees quickly migrated to military service. Although the park was available for public use, development was delayed until 1950, when dam construction began to impound the waters of a tributary of the Thompson River. The resulting lake partially filled three valleys of a heavily forested, steeply rolling landscape. On June 22, 1952, the park was formally dedicated, and development of camping, picnicking, fishing, boating, and beach facilities followed.

LELAND SEARLES

Today, facilities in the 1,119-acre park have expanded to include three campgrounds, one of them for equestrian use, and a modern, universally accessible family cabin. In addition to a 3.8-mile trail around the lake, several miles of multiple-use trails pass through stands of mature hardwoods and remnants of native prairie. The 64-acre lake, which drains a large watershed, was once on the state's list of impaired waters. However, in recent years, a series of lake restoration measures has significantly reduced the rate of sedimentation, improved water quality, and bolstered fish populations.

DON POGGENSEE

# Oak Grove State Park

In late 1925, the Hawarden Booster Club began floating the idea of a state park along the Big Sioux River in Sioux County. One meeting led to another, then another, and local interest turned into enthusiasm. By August of the following year, a committee had secured an option on a tract of rugged land along the eastern margins of the river valley, where a grove of native bur oaks grew. After Sioux County residents donated part of the purchase price, the Iowa State Board of Conservation agreed to fund the balance, and Oak Grove State Park was born.

In 1925, the county took steps to build a road to the park, but park improvements did not come until 1930, when the Board of Conservation erected a peeled-log picnic shelter (still in use). Additional improvements were made in 1934 by World War I veterans in the Civilian Conservation Corps, who planted seedling oak trees and built trails, enlarged the picnic area, and constructed a caretaker's residence (still in use but heavily altered).

Since 1962, the 101-acre park has been managed by the Sioux County Conservation Board under an agreement with the Iowa Department of Natural Resources. In addition to constructing two new shelters, an enclosed lodge, two campgrounds with related facilities, and a headquarters building, the county board, in 1967, also began purchasing adjacent land. The combined Oak Grove State Park–Big Sioux Park now covers 433 acres overlooking the Big Sioux River. The county board also conducts an extensive environmental education program, which in the near future will be housed in a new nature center in Big Sioux Park.

KEVIN KANE

DON CRAIG

# Okamanpedan State Park

Okamanpedan State Park takes its name from a Sioux word meaning "little nesting place of herons," as recorded by French explorer Jean-Nicolas Nicollet, who stopped at the lake now known as Tuttle Lake in Emmet County during his 1838 expedition to map the area between the Mississippi and Missouri Rivers. The Sioux called the lake Okamanpedan, and so the park was named when it was dedicated in 1926. The Iowa State Board of Conservation had identified this lake as a potential state park location in its 1919 report, and in 1923 brothers L. E. and J. C. Williams donated 10 acres of land along the south shore for this purpose.

The land included a cobblestone building known as Ellsworth Cottage, built in the late nineteenth century to serve as a hunting lodge on the 3,700-acre ranch of Eugene O. Ellsworth, benefactor of Ellsworth Community College. This little park is rich in Iowa history. At the dedication ceremony, the Estherville Chapter of the Daughters of the American Revolution unveiled a bronze tablet commemorating the park as the spot where Nicollet's party camped in 1838 and Major Thomas W. Sherman's party camped in 1860 as he moved his battery from Fort Leavenworth, Kansas, to Fort Ridgely, Minnesota.

Tuttle Lake, named for early settler Calvin Tuttle, straddles the Iowa-Minnesota border. It is a glacial lake, one of many left behind as the Des Moines Lobe ice sheet slowly melted about 12,000 years ago. The lowland landscape along the south shoreline is marked by an outlet channel, which is the source of the East Fork of the Des Moines River. Only a third of the 2,730-acre lake is on the Iowa side of the border, which caused a brief conflict with landowners on

KEVIN KANE

the Minnesota side when the Board of Conservation erected a dam on the river to maintain the lake at its ordinary high-water level.

In the mid-1920s, an access road was built and trees were planted in the park. Civilian Conservation Corps workers constructed a rubble stone bathhouse-concession building in 1934. Since then, the park has changed very little. The bathhouse-concession building now serves as a shelter house, as does the historic hunting lodge. Mature trees provide a shaded setting for picnics and shoreline fishing.

# Palisades-Kepler State Park | Palisades-Dows State Preserve

Along a bend in the Cedar River southwest of Mount Vernon lie the palisades, a recreational spot as well as an area of scientific interest long before the Iowa State Board of Conservation acquired the first 140 acres for a state park in 1922. Both geologists and sightseers were drawn to this stretch of river with its tree-topped cliffs of Silurian age dolomite. The weathered cliffs—an impressive cross section of sediments slowly built up from the floor of the tropical sea that covered much of the Midwest millions of years ago—held a rich record of fossilized marine life. Between the 1880s and 1920, two hotels and scores of private cottages were built along the palisades, and it was the site of Camp Iowar, a summer camp for boys and girls. During the 1920s and early 1930s, it was a favorite haunt of poet Carl Sandburg.

Linn County residents donated funds to pay half the cost of the initial 140 acres on the west side of the river. A large addition came in 1926, when attorney Louis Kepler willed 200 acres to the state; subsequently, the name was changed to Palisades-Kepler State Park. The state also acquired cottage lots and larger tracts on both sides of the river as they became available. Between 1933 and 1942, the east side of the river was developed. Civilian Conservation Corps workers built a large stone-and-timber lodge, an overlook shelter, three bridges, entrance portals, a low head dam in the river, and 5 miles of trails. In the early 1940s, a Works Progress Administration crew completed four small wooden cabins that were restored in 2004. Because land on the west side contained several uncommon plants and more than 125 species of birds had been observed there, the Iowa Conservation Commission determined that it would remain undeveloped as a wildlife preserve.

In 1962, Sutherland Dows, a businessman, civic leader, and philanthropist from Cedar Rapids, donated 150 acres of adjacent land on the west to the Linn County Conservation Board. Eighty acres of this tract plus 250 acres of state land were dedicated as Palisades-Dows State Preserve in 1980. The preserve's rugged terrain holds a large stand of mature oak-dominated forest, which provides secluded wildlife and bird habitat. Many species of ferns, liverworts, and mosses populate the dolomite cliffs, and very old eastern red cedars cling to the rock faces. Several rock shelters in ravines along the river provide evidence of Native American occupation during the Woodland period (800 BC–AD 1250).

The Native American past is also evident in several conical burial mounds in the park, which now covers 840 acres. Park visitors still view the river from the historic stone overlook shelter, and the historic lodge still accommodates large gatherings. Other park amenities include modern camping facilities, two open picnic shelters, four restored cabins, and nearly 6 miles of hiking trails. A boat launch on the Lower Palisades provides river access. The park also allows rock climbing, although climbers are required to sign a waiver.

# Pammel State Park

Louis Pammel's vision for Iowa's state park system is well reflected in the park that bears his name. As a leading conservationist, respected botanist at Iowa State University, and chair of the Iowa State Board of Conservation from its organization to 1927, Pammel guided development during the system's formative years. Although he valued outdoor recreation and was a pragmatist, he ardently championed parks as places to preserve native wildlife, plants, and trees; natural features that revealed Iowa's geological history; archaeological remains associated with American Indians; and buildings associated with Iowa's settlement history. Upon his death in 1931, the Board of Conservation proclaimed him "the most valuable single influence" in the conservation movement in Iowa. His holistic vision is a legacy embedded in Iowa's state park system.

The Board of Conservation purchased this rugged wooded tract along the Middle River in 1923 and 1924. Then called Devil's Backbone for a ridge of limestone that defines the river's twisting course, the park was renamed Pammel when it was dedicated in 1930. In the intervening years, development was restrained. Inmates from Anamosa State Penitentiary built a new park road, embellished with an iconic limestone tunnel that was created by enlarging and shoring up an old millrace, hand-dug in 1856 through the narrowest part of the backbone. Inmates also constructed a rustic log lodge from oak trees harvested in the park. During the 1930s, war veterans in the Civilian Conservation Corps constructed stone entrance portals and a picnic area with an open limestone-and-timber shelter.

To a large degree, the 350-acre park maintains the qualities that Louis Pammel held dear. All the historic structures are still in use, and new development has complemented the park's quiet nature. Five miles of trails wind along the ridge and through stands of old-growth forest. The meandering Middle River is a favorite with anglers and paddlers, and a ford across the river is a popular attraction for motorists and kids of all ages. The park's modest-size campground provides modern and nonmodern sites as well as two yurt cabins. A rural chapel acquired with a recent land addition has been converted into a nature center. Since 1989, the Madison County Conservation Board has managed the park under an agreement with the Iowa Department of Natural Resources.

# Pikes Peak State Park

Pikes Peak State Park in Clayton County offers a breathtaking view of the most storied region of Iowa. People have lived in the Upper Mississippi River valley for at least 13,000 years, using the Mississippi and Wisconsin Rivers as travel and trade routes. During the Woodland period (800 BC–AD 1250), American Indians buried their dead in ceremonial places, which included the high bluffs on the Iowa side of the river. On June 17, 1673, Father Jacques Marquette recorded sighting "a large chain of very high mountains" as he, fur trader Louis Joliet, and a party of voyageurs steered their canoes into the Mississippi at its confluence with the Wisconsin River.

French fur-trading posts soon appeared, initiating extensive trading networks with the Meskwaki and Ho-Chunk (Winnebago). In 1805, two years after the Louisiana Purchase, a U.S. military expedition led by Lieutenant Zebulon Pike set out to locate the source of the Mississippi and, along the way, passed the bluffs that now bear his name. Military forts replaced trading posts, providing some order to the forced relocation of the remaining Meskwaki and Ho-Chunk in advance of mass Euro-American settlement. In 1847, Alexander MacGregor platted a town along the river at the base of Pikes Peak.

Although Pikes Peak does not rival Zebulon Pike's other namesake in Colorado, it is one of the highest points along the Mississippi River, towering 500 feet above the water level. Downcutting and sculpting of the majestic river valley by repeated episodes of glacial meltwater floods exposed an intricate geological record of Cambrian age sandstones and Ordovician age dolomites, limestones, sandstones, and shales. The weathered bluffs are heavily forested; native sugar maple, red oak, white oak, and basswood dominate the steep rocky ravines, while white oak and shagbark hickory dominate the loess-covered, gently sloping summits.

In the early twentieth century, Pikes Peak was the focal point of a proposed national park. Toward that end, a descendant of Alexander MacGregor donated several tracts of land to the federal government in 1928. However, the National Park Service ultimately judged the proposal unworkable, and in 1936 Congress conveyed portions of the donated land to the state of Iowa for public use. These formed the core of two small state parks: Pikes Peak and Point Ann, close to each other but separated by privately owned land. The Iowa Conservation Commission built an access road, trails, and a stone combination concession and picnic shelter at Pikes Peak.

Land acquisitions finally joined Point Ann to Pikes Peak in the late 1960s. The park now covers 970 acres. Today, visitors especially enjoy the universally accessible picnic area and playground near the historic concession-shelter, with a panoramic blufftop overlook nearby and a boardwalk around Bear Mound, one of sixty-three Woodland period mounds in the park. An elaborate boardwalk system leads down a ravine to Bridal Veil Falls, a popular natural feature. Another 11 miles of hiking and multiple-use trails pass through old-growth forest, excellent for bird watching, and out to Point Ann. The park also includes a modern campground.

# Pilot Knob State Park | Pilot Knob State Preserve

"To the pioneer the boundless prairies of the Mississippi valley seem to have come ever with the irresistible suggestion of the sea. The endless meadows of dark grasses driven in waves before the wind established a more vivid likeness and . . . any natural object which aided the traveler to find his way across the unmarked plain became a 'pilot.'" So remarked Thomas Macbride in 1902 when he described the feature known as Pilot Knob, a conical mound of glacial debris left during melting of the Des Moines Lobe ice sheet. Macbride also noted that it was one of the finest examples of a glacial kame in the Upper Midwest and should become a park "for the delight and enjoyment of the people for all time."

Pilot Knob did become one of the earliest state parks. In 1921, local citizens donated about half of the park's original 238 acres, which in addition to the steep mound included forested uplands, several wetland marshes, and a small upland fen, also called Deadman's Lake, that supports a rare floating sphagnum mat. During the 1920s, the park was developed with a picnic shelter, caretaker's residence, park road, and trails. More extensive improvements came in 1934, when Civilian Conservation Corps workers built several structures in the distinctive rustic style. These included a 50-foot-tall stone observation tower atop the mound, an amphitheater, another picnic shelter, entrance portals, footbridges, and a wooden toboggan run. The CCC historic district is on the National Register of Historic Places.

Over the decades, park acreage has been gradually

CARL KURTZ

increased to its present size of 580 acres and further developed with a 15-acre artificial lake. In 1968, most of the original park was dedicated as a biological and geological state preserve to protect the upland fen and the abundance of plant species that thrive in the wetland and upland forest communities.

Native Americans ascribed significance to this prominent landmark, although exactly what is unknown. A total of twenty-six archaeological sites, mostly small scatters of prehistoric artifacts, have been documented in and adjacent to the park. Clustering of this many sites in an upland area away from a perennial river is unusual, and the presence of artifacts on top of the knob itself suggests that Native Americans sought out this prominence.

# Pine Lake State Park

The community of Eldora had its heart set on a lake when, in 1920, more than 150 individuals and businesses contributed nearly $19,000 and donated 29 acres toward the creation of a state park along the Iowa River in Hardin County. Although artificial lakes were not on the Iowa State Board of Conservation's agenda at the time, the location was of interest because the steep hills east of the river contained old-growth white pines, the southernmost native stand of this boreal species in Iowa. Thus, in 1922 and 1923, the waters of Pine Creek, a tributary of the Iowa River, were dammed to create the first artificial lake in an Iowa state park.

The steep hills, formed by the downcutting of Pine Creek through Pre-Illinoian glacial drift, exposed outcrops of Pennsylvanian age sandstone, which were quarried to construct a beachside concession building. Other recreational amenities built in the 1920s included a waterslide, a bandstand, and a boat concession. Privately owned land adjacent to the park on the north side became a golf course, a portion of which extended into the park, and many cottages popped up just beyond the park boundaries.

Between 1933 and 1935, the park was more extensively developed with the aid of Civilian Conservation Corps workers. Most important, a second lake—Upper Pine Lake—was constructed to help control siltation in Lower Pine Lake, the original lake. Additionally, CCC crews built check dams and planted 300,000 trees to help control soil erosion, constructed 6 miles of trails and ten footbridges, and quarried more sandstone to construct a stone-and-timber lodge overlooking Lower Pine Lake as well as four cabins between the lower lake and the Iowa River. For winter

JIM SCHEFFLER

recreation, a toboggan run was built from the hill behind the lodge to the lake. By the mid-1930s, Pine Lake State Park was a recreational gem.

In 1958, the dam at Upper Pine Lake was raised to alleviate the effects of ongoing siltation. This increased the size of the lake, and a new boat concession and a campground were added to the upper lake in the mid-1960s. Water quality, however, remains a continuing problem. A decade of rejuvenating the 668-acre park began in 1991, when Lower Pine Lake was drained, and the dam, which had been deemed unsafe, was rebuilt and raised. Two years later, the CCC-era cabins were renovated and modernized for year-round use. In 2000, the stone lodge was completely refurbished, and the beachside concession building was converted to an open picnic shelter. Community involvement also reemerged in the 1990s with the formation of the Friends of Pine Lake State Park, which raised funds to help restore the stone entrance portals.

JIM SCHEFFLER

153

# Pleasant Creek State Recreation Area

Open space for outdoor recreation sometimes comes from unlikely sources. As the large lakes program was getting underway in the late 1960s, Iowa Electric Light and Power Company of Cedar Rapids was also planning to construct a nuclear power generating station on the Cedar River near Palo. The plan included building a reservoir to assure an adequate flow of water for cooling purposes when the river was low. To implement this part of the plan, the power company approached the Iowa Conservation Commission with a proposal to construct the dam and an auxiliary pumping system if the ICC would acquire sufficient land and develop outdoor recreation facilities. It was an attractive opportunity for another lake-focused recreation area near an urban center. The two parties finalized an agreement in 1973, and land acquisition was completed in 1975, aided by federal matching grants through the Land and Water Conservation Fund.

Between 1978 and the late 1980s, Pleasant Creek was developed with a modern campground that includes four pine-log camping cabins, a beach complex, a day-use lodge, boat launches, and 8 miles of multiple-use trails. In 1991, the Iowa Department of Natural Resources began partnering with the Linn County Roads Department and several sporting organizations to reestablish tallgrass and shortgrass prairie communities on more than 400 acres. These habitats help maintain wildlife populations for hunters, who can use this portion of the recreation area during open seasons. A designated field trial area at the far south end is available for hunters to train dogs.

IOWA DNR

In 2014, the level of the 410-acre lake was lowered to line the shoreline with rock. This helps maintain the lake's excellent water quality, which attracts scuba divers in addition to windsurfers, paddlers, and anglers. On a side note, the power company has drawn lake water only once, in 1978, to augment the Cedar River flow. Since 2008, adequate water flow has been maintained through modifications to the river itself. The nuclear power plant, known as the Duane Arnold Energy Center, is scheduled to shut down in 2020.

# Prairie Rose State Park

Prairie Rose, one of the last artificial lake parks to be created in southern Iowa, has a thorny history befitting its name. This project had top priority when the legislature authorized funding for a series of artificial lakes in 1947, but construction was delayed while engineers studied a multitude of possible sites. In 1952, the Iowa Conservation Commission finally settled on this spot in the vicinity of a short-lived pioneer village known as Prairie Rose. However, the project was delayed several more years while the courts resolved land acquisition challenges. The dam, completed in 1960, created a 218-acre lake with an average depth of 10 feet and 7 miles of shoreline. It impounds drainage waters in the watershed of the east branch of the West Nishnabotna River. After the park was dedicated in 1962, the ICC planted trees and developed the grounds for picnicking, camping, boating, and fishing.

The park quickly became a popular outdoor recreation spot. Unfortunately, like many of Iowa's lakes, Prairie Rose did not have a watershed buffer sufficient to maintain water quality. Prairie Rose Lake was one of the first projects to receive funding through the 1979 Rural Clean Water Program, which helped farmers in the lake's 4,600-acre watershed implement conservation practices. This provided some benefits, but by 2000 sedimentation had reduced the lake's size, and water quality was impaired. The multiyear Prairie Rose Lake Water Quality Project, begun in 2008, was more effective. Funded by state and federal agencies in collaboration with private landowners, this project constructed more than 40 miles of terraces and many waterways on surrounding farms, and the

MIKE BYRNES

218-acre lake was reengineered to reduce the rate of sedimentation and provide fish habitats.

The water-quality project has helped sustain the park's popularity. Its 422 acres of parkland are well developed with modern and nonmodern camping facilities, picnic areas, boat launches and fishing piers, and a beachside recreation area. Seven miles of multiple-use trails attract hikers, bicyclists, snowmobilers, and cross-country skiers. Volunteers organized in 2011 as the Friends of Prairie Rose State Park to assist park staff with maintenance, improvements, and public programming.

157

# Preparation Canyon State Park

Preparation Canyon State Park takes its name from the now-vanished town of Preparation, founded in 1854 by Mormons who left the main group during its long trek from Nauvoo, Illinois, to Utah. Some fifty to sixty families chose to settle in western Iowa and "prepare" for the heavenly afterlife. Their farms covered several thousand acres, and the town once had nearly six hundred residents. The park includes the farm site of settlers Charles and Hannah Perrin, although no farm buildings remain.

"Canyon" calls attention to the deep valleys and gullies that alternate with high ridge crests throughout the steeply corrugated landscape of the Loess Hills, so named for the windblown deposits of loess that occur in a narrow band along 200 miles of the Missouri River valley in western Iowa. Most of these silt-rich deposits originated as glacial outwash carried down the river during summer melting of northern glaciers. During low-flow winters, silt was swept from the valley floodplain by strong west winds and deposited along the leeward margins, most recently between 27,000 and 13,000 years ago.

After the Iowa State Board of Conservation purchased 187 acres in Monona County as a "forest preserve" in 1935, Civilian Conservation Corps workers improved the tract with picnic areas and trails, which wind through the rugged hills and offer sweeping panoramic views of the broad Missouri River valley. In 1964, it was reclassified as a state park; however, it remains minimally developed in order to protect the fragile landscape. Ten hike-in camping sites not only reduce land disturbance but foster a quiet environment that makes the park a

JOHN PEARSON

favorite place for backpack camping. Now 544 acres in size, the park sits adjacent to the Preparation Canyon Unit of the Loess Hills State Forest, which provides additional protection. Both are on the Loess Hills National Scenic Byway.

DON CRAIG

# Red Haw State Park

Known for many years as Red Haw Hill State Park, this heavily wooded park is named for a variety of hawthorn tree that once grew abundantly here when the hillsides were more open. Today, the park is noted for an abundance of redbud trees. They cloak the landscape with pink blossoms each spring, but discerning eyes can still spot white-blossomed hawthorn trees here and there.

The park's origins are in the Great Depression, which was accompanied by widespread drought. In 1934, after the city of Chariton was forced to ship water in by rail, local residents raised money to purchase a tract of steeply rolling land drained by Little White Breast Creek. The city appealed to the Iowa Emergency Relief Administration for assistance in clearing trees and constructing a dam to impound the creek waters. Work began later that year with assistance through the Civilian Conservation Corps and, later, the Works Progress Administration. In 1936, when the artificial lake project was nearly complete, the city donated the site to the state, and the Iowa Conservation Commission agreed to develop it as a state park.

By 1940, park amenities included a large stone-and-timber picnic shelter on a hill overlooking the picturesque lake, several other picnic areas, a boat dock, and a "fishermen's" shelter. The 72-acre lake quickly became known as a good fishing lake and remains so today. In 1969, a fisheries research station was constructed near the dam. More picnic shelters were added in the 1970s, one of which was constructed by workers in the Young Adult Conservation Corps, a program modeled on the Civilian Conservation

LELAND SEARLES

Corps that offered young people conservation-related employment and educational opportunities. From 1977 to 1981, the Iowa Conservation Commission operated YACC camps at three locations: Red Haw and Big Creek State Parks and Yellow River State Forest.

In 1997, the park was enlarged by 229 acres to protect the lake from siltation; it now covers 649 acres. The new tract, where reconstructed prairie areas provide wildlife habitat, is open to seasonal hunting. In addition to the scenic no-wake lake and many picnic spots, the park also features a 4-mile multiple-use trail around the lake and a modern campground.

# Rice Lake State Park

Rice Lake State Park in Winnebago County has a larger story than its small size would suggest. In 1906, despite considerable local opposition, state authorities decided to drain Rice Lake and sell the land for agricultural use. The lake covered about 1,200 acres: 500 acres of open water of varying depths, the rest marshy. Wild rice and other grasses grew in abundance, providing habitat for many species of fish, waterfowl, and fur-bearing mammals. A number of private summer cottages had been built along the south shore, where the water was deeper.

Had the drainage effort succeeded, the story would have ended there. But the level terrain of the lakebed wetlands, formed 15,000 to 12,000 years ago during melting episodes of the Des Moines Lobe glacier, could not be adequately drained. The project simply reduced the size of the lake and marsh and produced no usable farmland. Passage of the State Park Act in 1917 sparked a new local initiative to reclaim the lake. In 1923, the Rice Lake Outing Club of Lake Mills purchased land for recreational use and, in 1924, granted the state access to some of the land as "open park land" on the condition that the Iowa State Board of Conservation take measures to restore the lake. The state agreed and purchased an additional 33 acres to create a state park on the south shore. In 1977, the land was deeded to the state.

Another condition appears to have been allowing a golf course to be laid out on parkland (much later, in 1977, the golf course was transferred to private ownership through a land trade agreement). The park itself occupied a wooded area next to the lake, and in 1934 Civilian Conservation Corps workers

erected a rustic stone-and-log picnic shelter there. With the aid of federal funds, forthcoming in 1941, the Iowa Conservation Commission began the process of restoring the lake by constructing a series of dikes to impound rainwater and a spillway to maintain the water level. The project, essentially completed in 1948, eventually re-created the wetland complex to its original size. Rice Lake State Park, now about 15 acres in size, showcases the historic picnic shelter, and the lake and marsh provide open water for fishing and boating as well as marshlands for bird watching and hunting. The park also protects archaeological remains associated with Middle Woodland to Late Prehistoric peoples (200 BC–AD 1600).

WARREN TERPSTRA

# Rock Creek State Park

Public clamor for artificial lake parks rebounded after World War II, in part because organized outdoor recreation groups redoubled their efforts. The origins of Rock Creek are a case in point. In early 1946, Newton's Emerson Hough Chapter of the Izaak Walton League met with Governor Robert Blue and the Iowa Conservation Commission to propose construction of a 1,500-acre lake surrounded by a 3,800-acre state park between Newton and Grinnell in Jasper County. That proposal made its way into a 1947 legislative appropriation to develop more artificial lakes in the southern part of the state. Construction of the dam to impound the waters of Rock Creek began in 1950, by which time the project had been scaled back to about half its proposed size. Still, when the park was dedicated on August 24, 1952, the 640-acre lake was the largest artificial lake in Iowa at the time. The immense flood-control reservoirs were still to come. Land acquisitions eventually resulted in a park of about 1,700 acres total.

The Iowa Conservation Commission developed the park with a campground, a picnic shelter and other picnic facilities, a beach house and concession building, and five boat launches. The size of the lake and its proximity to Highway 6 and, later, Interstate 80, construction of which was completed between Des Moines and the Iowa-Illinois border in 1966, helped make Rock Creek one of the most popular state parks for camping and boating, and it remains so today. The two hundred–site campground includes modern facilities, a playground, a fish-cleaning station, courtesy docks, and a boat ramp. Boat rentals and dock slips are available at the concession building.

MARLYS POPMA

Additionally, 8.5 miles of multipurpose trails are available for hiking, horseback riding, mountain biking, snowmobiling, and cross-country skiing.

The size of the lake's watershed, nearly 27,000 acres, has been a challenge. By the time the park turned fifty, the lake had shrunk to less than 500 acres, and water quality was poor. This was the catalyst for a multifaceted effort to slow the rate of sedimentation and reduce nutrient levels. The Iowa Department of Natural Resources added catch basins within the park and acquired additional land northwest of the park for wildlife habitat as well as natural filtration. Federal, state, and county agencies collaborated to conduct a comprehensive assessment of watershed hot spots and areas exhibiting sound conservation practices, followed by the production of detailed maps displaying problem areas and the potential for improvement. This preceded an ongoing process of working with landowners to expand private land and water conservation efforts throughout the watershed.

# Sharon Bluffs State Park

In the late 1920s, investigating a stretch of bluffs along the Chariton River in Appanoose County as a possible state park site, the Iowa State Board of Conservation found that there was local interest in assisting with such an effort. A plan began to take shape in 1929 when a group of business associates from Centerville approached the board with a proposal. Two years later, the state purchased heavily wooded land on both sides of the river. Steep clay and shale outcroppings rise from the east bank to form bluffs that overlook a floodplain along the west side of the river. In accordance with park-naming guidelines adopted by the Iowa Conservation Commission in 1935, which called for descriptive names defining the character of the area, the park was named Sharon for an early settlement in the vicinity and Bluffs for the park's primary natural feature.

During the 1930s, Civilian Conservation Corps workers created trails, picnic areas, and a parking area. CCC crews also constructed a large stone-and-timber shelter house on top of the bluffs, with a massive fireplace and a lovely view of the Chariton River valley below. The shelter house was renovated in 1998.

Since 1981, the 144-acre park has been managed by the Appanoose County Conservation Board under an agreement with the Iowa Department of Natural Resources. In 2000, the County Conservation Board constructed a nature center, which houses an extensive collection of mounted wildlife. It also offers day camps and educational programs at the center. Other amenities at this peaceful park include a small campground, boat access to the river, and wooded hiking trails.

# Springbrook State Park

As new state parks were established in the early 1920s, Iowans quickly discovered their social as well as economic benefits, and many communities began to investigate the prospects for a state park in their particular area. So it was that in 1925 the Guthrie Center Rotary Club consulted with Louis Pammel about the possibility of a state park along the Middle Raccoon River, where land was available. Pammel was impressed with the site, and the Rotary Club began fund-raising to help pay part of the purchase price. By mid-1926, the towns of Panora, Bagley, Bayard, Yale, and Guthrie Center had all chipped in, and the Iowa State Board of Conservation agreed to pay the balance.

The 950-acre park was extensively developed by Civilian Conservation Corps workers in the 1930s. Structures that remain include stone entrance portals, a rustic stone-and-log picnic shelter, a small artificial lake with a beach area and large bathhouse, and a stable that was later converted to park offices. CCC crews also constructed eight cabins as part of a planned group camp before World War II intervened. After the war, the Iowa Conservation Commission finished the project by remodeling three CCC barracks for use as a recreation hall, a dining hall, and a shower-bathroom building. Only the eight cabins remain.

From 1950 to 1984, Iowa State Teachers College (now the University of Northern Iowa) operated the Iowa Teachers Conservation Camp at Springbrook, a summer program where teachers could earn college credit for conservation education courses. The program was housed in the group camp until 1971, when the new Springbrook Conservation Education

JOHN PEARSON

Center opened, a four-building complex designed to serve conservation education activities year-round by groups from throughout the state. However, as county conservation boards increasingly embraced environmental education as part of their mission, the need for a statewide center waned, and the Iowa Department of Natural Resources closed the Conservation Education Center in 2017.

The picturesque Middle Raccoon River cuts through the park's southern area, exposing outcrops of sandstone from the Cretaceous period. Twelve miles of hiking trails run through the hilly, heavily wooded park. In addition to the swimming beach, park amenities include picnic areas, a large modern campground, a large year-round rental house, fishing facilities on the river as well as the artificial lake, and seasonal hunting in marked areas. The Central State Bike Route connects Springbrook with Ledges and Big Creek State Parks via lightly traveled county highways.

# Stone State Park | Mount Talbot State Preserve

Located in the northern reach of the Loess Hills within the city limits of Sioux City, Stone State Park and Mount Talbot State Preserve provide urbanites with easy access to a large natural area that feels remarkably remote. The names Stone and Talbot refer to local citizens linked to the history of the land. In 1885, real estate tycoon Daniel H. Talbot, also an amateur naturalist of some renown, purchased what later became core parkland. After Talbot lost his fortune in the Panic of 1893, banker Thomas Jefferson Stone acquired the property. His son, Edgar, began developing the land for use as a park. After Edgar's death, the city of Sioux City acquired the property from the Stone family in 1912 and continued to develop it as a park and zoo.

In 1935, the state purchased the park from the city, and the Iowa Conservation Commission began extensive improvements to expand recreational use. Between 1935 and 1939, Civilian Conservation Corps crews built picnic and camping areas, several park buildings, an ice-skating rink, and toboggan and ski runs. The winter sports facilities and the zoo were removed in the early 1940s, but many historic structures remain, including a rustic stone-and-timber day-use lodge, the Calumet picnic shelter complex, and stone entrance portals.

The 1,595-acre park is a popular picnicking, camping, and gathering spot. There are more than 12 miles of scenic trails through rugged Loess Hills terrain and several ridgetop overlooks with extraordinary views of the Big Sioux and Missouri

JOHN PEARSON

River valleys. In 1995, the Dorothy Pecaut Nature Center opened on the south edge of the park. Owned and operated by the Woodbury County Conservation Board, the center features outstanding exhibits on Loess Hills geology and natural history, several short trails, and butterfly and wildflower gardens.

Mount Talbot State Preserve is so named for the high grassy ridge at the park's northern end on what was once Daniel Talbot's land. Floristic surveys conducted by The Nature Conservancy and the Iowa Department of Natural Resources led to this 90-acre area being dedicated as a biological preserve in 1989. A more recent survey identified 389 species of native vascular plants in the park and preserve.

DON POGGENSEE

171

# Swan Lake State Park

Swan Lake represents one of the earliest examples of reconstituting a historic wetland. Drainage from the melting margins of the Des Moines Lobe ice sheet left outwash deposits of gravel and extensive wetlands. Situated among the early drainageways of the Middle Raccoon River, Swan Lake was one of them. In 1933, with assistance from the Carroll Chamber of Commerce and Senator I. G. "Jack" Chrystal, who secured a legislative appropriation, the Iowa State Board of Conservation began purchasing tracts that included the wetland. From 1934 through 1938, various federal relief programs funded workers who constructed a dam to create a shallow lake, planted trees, and built a park road, picnic area, shelter house, and trails.

In 1955, when the Iowa Conservation Commission was struggling to manage a system that was underfunded in relation to growing public demand for outdoor recreation, it transferred management of Swan Lake to the Carroll County Wildlife Conservation League. This agreement prefigured passage of the 1955 state law authorizing voters to create county conservation boards and levy local taxes for park funds. In 1958, the newly created Carroll County Conservation Board assumed park management responsibilities.

The county board added boating, fishing, and camping facilities, a sand beach, and an enclosed shelter house. After the state purchased an adjacent farm in 1967, an exhibit of live animals and birds, established by the Junior Chamber of Commerce, was moved into existing farm structures. In 1971, the Carroll County Historical Society converted the

barn into the Farmstead Museum. Today, the park covers 510 acres, including the 110-acre lake, which between 1981 and 1985 was reengineered to improve water quality and restore fisheries. In 1986, the Iowa Conservation Commission constructed a universally accessible, all-weather fishing shelter, the first of its kind in the state. In 1990, work began on the Sauk Rail Trail, a 33-mile multiple-use trail that now connects Black Hawk and Swan Lake State Parks.

Over the years, the wildlife exhibit came to include exotic animals, including a chimpanzee named Elvis who proved to be an escape artist. Although the exhibit was popular, it was also controversial, and in 1992 the Iowa Natural Resources Commission adopted guidelines requiring that wildlife exhibits be limited to native species displayed for educational purposes in natural habitats. Thus began a transition that resulted in a state-of-the-art conservation education center, which opened in 2004. The center was completely funded with private contributions and local in-kind donations.

# Twin Lakes State Park

Senator Perry C. Holdoegel, who was instrumental in passing the 1917 State Park Act, also played a key role in establishing this small state park in his home district. In 1921, local citizens first presented their proposal for a state park at North Twin Lake, the deeper of two side-by-side natural lakes in Calhoun County. The shoreline, however, was completely held by private landowners, and no parcels were for sale. Holdoegel repeatedly appeared before the Iowa State Board of Conservation to advocate for a state park somewhere on the lake. After negotiations to purchase land failed, the state finally took extreme measures in 1923 and condemned 15 acres of land known as Sandy Point, which included 500 feet of shoreline. A few more acres northeast of Sandy Point were purchased in 1924, providing a second area of public access to the lake.

The Board of Conservation planted trees, but other planned improvements were delayed until 1934, when Civilian Conservation Corps workers constructed a large stone-and-log shelter house at Sandy Point, now called the East Area. Over the years, other amenities have been added, including beaches, playgrounds, and open picnic shelters at both units, boat ramps, and a 7-mile paved multiple-use trail around the 453-acre North Twin Lake.

North and South Twin Lakes are glacial lakes created when the Des Moines Lobe melted about 13,000 years ago. A narrow strip of land separates the two bodies of water. The shallow waters of South Twin Lake cover about 600 acres, which the Iowa Department of Natural Resources manages as a wildlife area. The north half of South Twin Lake is

DON POGGENSEE

designated as a wildlife refuge, while public hunting in season is permitted in the south half.

DON POGGENSEE

175

# Union Grove State Park

As unemployment rose during the Great Depression, many communities proposed public works projects to attract federal work relief funds. This is what led Tama County to revive an old idea for a rural park in 1935 and seek the advice of the Iowa Conservation Commission in choosing a location. The ICC judged that a spot known as Union Grove would be ideal because the waters of Deer Creek could be dammed to create an artificial lake, and it was central to residents of both Tama and Marshall Counties. To generate local support, a nonprofit organization, the Lake and Park Holding Corporation, sold $100 membership certificates to raise $35,000 for land acquisition. The face value of the certificates could then be applied to the purchase of private lots near the lake. A promising location and ample local support helped secure Works Progress Administration funding to create the lake.

In 1936, WPA workers constructed most of the dam, although the work was finished by a private contractor. The dam's spillway creates a tranquil waterfall, one of the park's main features. After the lake filled, the corporation began selling cottage lots, but financial shortfalls prevented park development beyond a beach and a bathhouse. To eliminate its debt, the corporation sold the 160-acre lake and 100 acres of surrounding land to the state for $10,000 in 1940.

World War II put the brakes on park development, and thereafter development was gradual. Service buildings were constructed in the early 1950s, and an open picnic shelter and a tent campground were added in the early 1960s. By the early 1970s, however, soil erosion had reduced the lake to less than 120 acres, and water quality was seriously impaired.

JIM SCHEFFLER

With prodding as well as assistance from the corporation, still in existence, federal and state agencies began working with private landowners to improve land and water management practices. Dredging operations were conducted in the early 1970s and again in the late 1980s. More extensive lake improvements took place between 2010 and 2017, when the Iowa Department of Natural Resources drained, dredged, and reengineered the lake. In partnership with the Iowa Natural Heritage Foundation, the DNR acquired an additional 110 acres of land north of the lake for watershed protection.

Union Grove remains a quiet, mostly day-use park, but lake improvement led to a renaissance, much of it accomplished with community assistance. Today, visitors find trails throughout the park and a completely modernized campground. Two boat launches and several fish jetties accommodate anglers; two year-round rental cabins attract family vacationers; and a playground beckons children. In 2005, the Lake and Park Holding Corporation received the DNR's Outstanding Group Volunteer Award for its decades of park support.

JIM SCHEFFLER

177

S. C. HARGIS

# Viking Lake State Park

Viking Lake was one of several artificial lake projects approved by the legislature in 1947 to meet the demand for lake-based outdoor recreation. In this case, hunters and anglers in southwest Iowa, initially represented by the Montgomery County Conservation League, lobbied for a lake, and legislators were supportive. A suitable site was quickly identified east of Stanton, where the waters of Dunns Creek could be impounded within the steeply rolling terrain. However, rising costs for engineering, materials, and labor forced the Iowa Conservation Commission to request supplemental appropriations four times in order to complete all eight projects. As a result, land acquisition did not begin until 1955, and dam construction was delayed until 1956.

Throughout the planning stages, the lake was referred to as Stanton Lake. Once construction was underway, however, the *Stanton Viking* newspaper initiated a contest to come up with a permanent name. When the park was dedicated on October 13, 1957, it was christened Viking Lake as a tribute to the many Scandinavians who had settled in the surrounding area. The lake opened for fishing in March 1959.

Public demand proved to be genuine. The thousand-acre park became a popular southwest Iowa destination, particularly for camping and fishing. A shady lakeshore campground offers more than a hundred large campsites with upgraded utilities, a playground, a day-use shelter with enclosed kitchenette, and a fish-cleaning station. The lake's irregular shoreline creates many coves and fingers for anglers. Four boat ramps and six universally accessible fishing jetties provide lake access at many points.

IOWA DNR

Other park amenities include more than 6 miles of trails, three picnic areas, and a beachside seasonal day-use lodge overlooking the lake.

# Volga River State Recreation Area

Frog Hollow Lake, which sits quietly in the northern part of this scenic recreation area, gives no hint of the political skirmishes that led to its creation. When the large lakes initiative was launched in 1967, the Volga River in Fayette County was one of three projects to receive initial state funding. Although the location was not near a major urban center, there were enthusiastic local supporters and powerful advocates in the state legislature. Land acquisition proceeded smoothly. However, geologists warned that the underlying bedrock was fractured and porous, making it unlikely that a reservoir would hold water. Thus, the original plan for a 1,680-acre lake was scaled back multiple times, and in 1970 the Iowa Conservation Commission decided to move the proposed dam to a tributary, Frog Hollow Creek, and impound a much smaller volume of water.

When the commission asked the legislature for additional money to fund engineering studies, it touched off years of fierce debate among legislators as well as between the legislature and the commission. Then, engineering studies confirmed the geologists' warnings, and the ICC voted to drop the lake from its development plan. The state legislature, however, put it back in. Ultimately, Frog Hollow Lake—138 acres—was a compromise between nature and politics. Construction of the lake, which began in 1978, required costly earthmoving to line the lakebed with a thick sealing layer of clay.

Settling the lake question opened the way to a different development concept, which focused on the basics. More than 20 miles of multiple-use trails accommodate equestrians, hikers, mountain bikers,

JOHN PEARSON

and cross-country skiers. In the late 1990s, modern camping facilities were constructed on the east side of the lake, but most of the nearly 5,700-acre recreation area remains in a natural state, typical of the rugged terrain associated with northeast Iowa. Anglers can enjoy a no-swimming and no-wake lake. Canoers and kayakers can paddle 7 miles of the Volga River as it winds through timbered canyons and craggy outcroppings. Public hunting is allowed in season, and wildlife populations are maintained through an ecosystem management plan that involves local farmers leasing several hundred acres to produce food and ground cover for multiple species.

# Walnut Woods State Park

In 1925, the Iowa State Board of Conservation identified this heavily wooded tract along the Raccoon River near Des Moines as a desirable state park location. Two years later, the state acquired the site from the Ben F. Elbert family, with the cities of Des Moines and Valley Junction as well as Polk County contributing nearly half the purchase price. For several years, it was known as Elbert State Park, honoring the prominent Des Moines businessman who had died in a tragic accident in 1905. However, in 1933 it was renamed Walnut Woods for the magnificent grove of black walnut trees growing there.

Picnic areas were created in the park, but it remained lightly used until 1932, when a new road made access easier. Between 1933 and 1936, crews from two Civilian Conservation Corps camps deepened an old channel of the Raccoon River to create a 20-acre lake, stabilized the banks of the river, built trails, and began constructing park buildings. After the CCC camps were moved elsewhere, workers hired through the Works Progress Administration finished developing the park. With the ability to hire skilled workers through the WPA, the Iowa Conservation Commission improvised a workshop at Walnut Woods. Carpenters hewed park benches and chairs from fallen trees. Metalworkers fabricated ornamental fixtures and hardware from scrap metal. Most notably, the dressed limestone of the stately lodge displays the work of skilled masons.

Riverbank stabilization has been an ongoing project, but around 1950 the Iowa Conservation Commission stopped maintaining the lake and allowed vegetation to take over. The lodge, which has

LINDA MACBRIDE

become the park's focal point, was renovated in 1995 after sustaining flood damage in 1993. Other amenities in the 261-acre park include a small but modern campground, redesigned to withstand flooding, shaded picnic areas throughout, and access to the Raccoon River for fishing and white-water paddling through the rapids known as Commerce Ledges.

The park is also a favorite spot for cross-country skiing and bird watching, with more than ninety species of birds observed from the bird blind and the 2.5 miles of trails that run through the woods and along the river. In 2017, under an agreement with the Des Moines Water Works, the Iowa Department of Natural Resources assumed management of Purple Martin Lake, named for an established colony of purple martins. Located west of Walnut Woods on the south side of the Raccoon River, this 214-acre former gravel pit, with an 87-acre lake, is open for low-impact recreation activities.

# Wapsipinicon State Park

Wapsipinicon State Park contains several features constructed in the 1920s, a major reason the park's historic core is listed on the National Register of Historic Places. In late 1920, the Iowa State Board of Conservation began investigating potential park locations along the Wapsipinicon River in Jones County. Coincidentally—or perhaps not—a committee of Anamosa business owners and farmers became keenly interested in having a state park nearby. Events happened quickly, and by late March 1921, the committee had purchased a tract of about 170 acres south of Anamosa along the river and donated it to the state.

The park's scenic quality comes from weathered exposures of Silurian age dolomite lining the Wapsipinicon River and Dutch Creek, which flow through the southern half of the park. The picturesque bluffs and steep slopes are marked by numerous pits, ledges, and crevices covered with mosses, lichens, liverworts, and ferns. Several small caves near Dutch Creek lend intrigue to the landscape, a reminder of the long-term effects of groundwater movement through these lime-rich rocks. Old-growth deciduous forest covers the park's west and north areas. The lower park road loops through a plantation of white pines established in the 1920s.

Clifford Niles, a banker and businessman from Anamosa who served on the Iowa State Board of Conservation from 1923 to 1927, played a prominent role in both land acquisition and park development. Inmates from Anamosa State Penitentiary provided the labor. In 1921, they constructed park roads, planted pine trees on a former agricultural field, and created picnic areas and a campground. Between 1922 and 1924, they laid out a nine-hole public golf course on a high bluff next to the campground, constructed a peeled-log community building, and fashioned entrance piers from boulders. The golf course, one of three that the Board of Conservation reluctantly allowed in state parks, is still in use, as is the community building. In 1927, a log cabin, known as the Boy Scouts Lodge, was added to the campground.

Other noteworthy 1920s features still present include a stone gateway flanking the common entrance to the upper and lower park roads, a stone pumphouse, two stone arch bridges over Dutch Creek, and a concrete creek ford known as the Upside Down Bridge. Because the park was considered fully developed by the late 1920s, it has no Depression era features, which contributes to its distinctive rustic character. Use of prison labor continued into the 1950s for maintenance and repair, construction of a park manager's residence and service buildings, and replacement of the Boy Scouts Lodge at the campground.

Incremental land acquisitions have extended the park across the river and also farther south, where public hunting is allowed. Today, the park encompasses 400 acres. The community has remained an active partner, assisting with construction of a day-use lodge and relocation of an 1879 three-span, bowstring-arch bridge now used as a pedestrian bridge across the Wapsipinicon River. Other park features include a modernized campground, a playground, picnic shelters, a footbridge over Dutch Creek, 3.5 miles of multiple-use trails, and two boat ramps on the river.

DON CRAIG

# Waubonsie State Park

Anchoring the southern end of the Loess Hills, Waubonsie State Park protects nearly 2,000 acres of this uncommon landscape. The terrain is composed primarily of silt that originated as glacial outwash carried down the Missouri River when glaciers melted to the north. During winter's seasonal low flows, strong westerly winds scoured silt from the river's broad floodplain and deposited it along the eastern side of the Missouri River valley, most recently between 27,000 and 13,000 years ago. Subsequent erosion of these deep deposits has carved them into the intricate shapes and patterns that characterize the Loess Hills today.

In 1926, a group of citizens from nearby Hamburg approached the Iowa State Board of Conservation and proposed to assist with the purchase of 200 acres of outstanding woodlands and grasslands. The seller, C. E. Mincer, then served as the park's first caretaker. Dedicated in 1930, the park is named for the Potawatomi leader who signed the 1833 treaty ceding lands in Indiana and Illinois in exchange for a "permanent" settlement along the Missouri River in southwestern Iowa. Chief Waubonsie died here in about 1848, after which the Potawatomi were moved, again, to their present-day reservation in Kansas.

During the 1930s, Civilian Conservation Corps workers built park roads, miles of trails, a large peeled-log picnic shelter, two toadstool-shaped shelters, campfire rings and seats, water fountains, a caretaker's residence, and a park maintenance building. Crews hired under the Works Progress Administration built footbridges and the park entrance portals. The original part of the park, which features a spectacular

JOHN PEARSON

view of the broad Missouri River floodplain, still looks much as it did in the 1930s.

Over the years, the park has been greatly expanded, the most recent acquisition being the 646-acre property known as Camp Wa-Shawtee of the Great Plains Girl Scout Council of Omaha. The camp staff's living quarters were converted to eight rental cabins (four seasonal and four year-round) and the nature center to a year-round day-use lodge. Seven-acre Lake Virginia attracts paddlers and anglers. Eight miles of multiple-use trails take visitors through oak-dominated woodlands and openings of native prairie. The park is on the Loess Hills National Scenic Byway. It is also a site on the Lewis and Clark National Historic Trail.

# Wildcat Den State Park | Fairport State Recreation Area

Before Wildcat Den became a state park, sisters Emma and Clara Brandt purchased, in 1905, a rugged tract near the family homestead. The intent was to preserve places already popular for picnicking and exploring: Steamboat Rock, Devil's Punch Bowl, and Fat Man's Squeeze. Naturalists also came here to study plants found in association with the varied topography and geology of Pine Creek valley. The creek cuts through glacial deposits of Illinoian age into Pennsylvanian age sandstone and finally, at the base of the bluffs, into limestone and shale of Devonian age. These differences in geologic materials and the proximity of this park to the nearby gorge of the Mississippi River result in scenic terrain and variable habitats. To protect the area from vandalism, the Brandt sisters hired a watchman.

REECE THOMPSON

After passage of the 1917 State Park Act, the Greater Muscatine Committee and the Brandt sisters sought to have the Iowa State Board of Conservation acquire the area for a state park. It took a few years for a plan to take effect, but in 1927 the board purchased 141 acres, including the historic Pine Creek Grist Mill, and the Brandts donated 67 acres. A few years later, the sisters also donated their 70-acre homestead.

The park holds a fascinating mix of cultural and natural history. In addition to displaying millions of years of geologic history, its varied topography supports more than 500 plant species and preserves fragments of native forest dominated by white and red oaks. The focal point is Pine Creek Grist Mill, built in 1848 and operated by successive owners until about 1920. The mill and a nearby bridge—an unaltered through-truss bridge erected in 1878 to serve wagon traffic to and from the mill—are both listed on the National Register of Historic Places. In the 1960s, the historic 1887 Melpine School was moved into the park. The Friends of Pine Creek Grist Mill have restored the mill and operate it in conjunction with interpretive programs. Likewise, the Friends of Melpine School have restored the building and occasionally conduct living history programs there.

More than 4 miles of trails loop through the 425-acre park. Only nonmodern camping is provided in the park itself, but modern campground facilities are available at Fairport State Recreation Area, 5 miles away overlooking the Mississippi River.

189

# Wilson Island State Recreation Area

Wilson Island's fascinating story is part of the environmental history of the Missouri River and the politics of state boundaries. To start with, Wilson Island is not an island, although it was once a large sandbar until the meandering Missouri River attached it to the Iowa side during one of its many changes of course. The name Wilson refers to former Iowa governor George A. Wilson, who served from 1939 to 1943 when the Iowa-Nebraska Boundary Compact was being formulated.

The compact sought to establish a permanent boundary between Iowa and Nebraska by drawing a line down the middle of the river as it existed at that time. But the river just kept on shifting. By the mid-1950s, U.S. Army Corps of Engineers flood-control projects had more or less contained the river, but not before a disastrous flood in 1952 produced significant course changes, which tossed the 1943 compact into a legal gray area. Iowa and Nebraska subsequently fought over border territory in the courts until 1972, when the U.S. Supreme Court decided ownership of thirty-two disputed land claims, including Wilson Island.

Meanwhile, the Iowa Conservation Commission began developing recreation areas on the Iowa side of the river. Wilson Island, then just 35 acres in size, was minimally developed as a game refuge in the 1950s. Then, in the mid-1960s, under a cost-sharing agreement, the Corps of Engineers constructed a boat ramp, camping pads, parking areas, and access roads; the Iowa Conservation Commission added group shelters, picnic tables and grills, utilities, and landscaping. Also in the mid-1950s, the U.S. Fish and Wildlife Service acquired more than 8,000

DON POGGENSEE

acres adjacent to Wilson Island on the north to create DeSoto National Wildlife Refuge. Thus, by 1972, Wilson Island was part of a well-established recreation area, and the Supreme Court decision affirmed Iowa's ownership.

Wilson Island has a spacious modern campground under a tall "cottonwood cathedral," with two youth group camping areas. Abundant wildlife, especially waterfowl, and access to the Missouri River are the major draws of this 544-acre recreation area. Picnic sites along the river invite day use, as do 6 miles of multiple-use trails that wind along the river and alongside a backwater chute on the east side. Wilson Island is also on the Lewis and Clark National Historic Trail.

# State Preserves

The State Preserves Act of 1965 authorized the Iowa Conservation Commission to designate areas of "unusual flora, fauna, geological, archaeological, scenic or historic features of scientific or educational value" as preserves that would receive the highest level of protection. As of 1965, only six other states had taken this step—Wisconsin, Illinois, Michigan, New Jersey, Virginia, and North Carolina—but they represented an emerging national concern for protecting native species and natural areas. During the Johnson administration, Congress passed three important federal laws to address this concern: the 1964 Wilderness Act, the 1966 Endangered Species Preservation Act, and the 1968 Wild and Scenic Rivers Act. A related measure, the 1966 National Historic Preservation Act, reflected an urgency to preserve the nation's historic buildings and antiquities from destruction in the face of unprecedented urban growth and interstate highway expansion. In passing the State Preserves Act, Iowa was in step with the growing environmental movement. Iowa also went a step further than other states by allowing cultural areas—archaeological and historic sites—as well as natural areas to be designated as state preserves.

Taking a longer view, natural scientists in Iowa began pressing for preserves in the 1920s after it became clear that all state parks would be open to recreational use. In 1927, the Iowa Academy of Science's Conservation Committee urged the Iowa State Board of Conservation to set aside areas to "serve as sanctuaries for the remnants of our native plant and animal life for scientific and general conservation purposes." That same year, the board designated Woodman Hollow in Webster County as "a reserve for the full protection of plant and animal life therein." Similarly, in 1934, when the board acquired the first 80 acres of White Pine Hollow in Dubuque County, they were designated as a forest preserve. The 1933 Iowa Twenty-five Year Conservation Plan observed that when the state acquired lands for parks, two objectives were often difficult to reconcile: "to preserve the character of the site" and to allow public recreational use that would "not seriously injure the natural character of the site." Accordingly, the plan recommended a dual system of parks and preserves that would allow light recreation in preserves and more intensive recreation in parks. This recommendation was not implemented, but in

1941, when the Iowa Conservation Commission first established formal categories, two of them implied a special status: "geologic-biologic parks and historical-archaeological monuments."

Mounting concern over the nearly total loss of Iowa's native prairie also shaped thinking about the need for state preserves. In 1934, botanist Bohumil Shimek proposed a large prairie preserve in the Little Sioux River valley, and Iowa Conservation Commission member Margo Frankel approached a private party about donating a large tract west of Lake Okoboji; neither of these attempts bore fruit. In the mid-1940s, the Iowa Academy of Science's Conservation Committee once again took the lead by commissioning botanist Ada Hayden to investigate remnants of native prairie and evaluate their floristic integrity.

Hayden was the foremost expert on prairie ecology in Iowa at the time. She had studied botany with Louis Pammel at Iowa State University, earning her doctorate in 1918—further distinguished as being the first woman to receive a doctoral degree from Iowa State—and then joining the faculty there. Her doctoral dissertation was on the ecology of prairie plants in central Iowa, and a year later, in 1919, she issued the first explicit call for the "Conservation of Prairie" in *Iowa Parks: Conservation of Iowa Historic, Scenic and Scientific Areas.* After observing that "the goddess of agriculture" had all but "banished the prairie," she rhetorically asked, "Should this bit of Eden be preserved only in literature?" Her proposal: to "preserve a few acres in each county . . . without encroaching on economic products" in order to save

patches of Iowa's prairie heritage for all time.

By the 1940s, native prairie relicts were harder to find. One of the remnants Hayden investigated, in the company of commission member Louise Lange Parker, was a 240-acre tract in Howard County, which the commission purchased in 1945. The commission also asked Hayden to prepare a report of her findings to guide the acquisition of other native prairie areas. She produced two reports, one published in 1945, the other in 1946, which identified more than twenty specific tracts. This led to the 1948 purchase of the Kalsow Prairie in Pocahontas County. Hayden died in 1950, before prairie preservation really took off; however, her reports set a precedent of using scientific studies to help make informed decisions about land acquisition.

In 1955, the commission adopted a new classification scheme, and fifteen areas were designated as state preserves, but there were no real guidelines for preserve status or management. Once again, the nudge forward came from elsewhere. The 1964 *Report on Iowa's Outdoor Resources*, ordered by Governor Harold Hughes, contained specific recommendations for legislation to authorize a system of state preserves. Modeled in part on laws passed in Illinois and Wisconsin, Iowa's State Preserves Act of 1965 stipulated that preserves be created from existing state-owned areas or from donations. It also authorized the creation of a State Preserves Advisory Board under the jurisdiction of the Iowa Conservation Commission, now the Iowa Department of Natural Resources. The advisory board is charged with recommending areas for dedication as state preserves, promoting research on existing and proposed preserves, negotiating management agreements for each preserve based on its significant features, and overseeing preserve management. As a tribute to Ada Hayden, the Howard County prairie tract was named in her honor when it was designated as a state preserve in May 1968.

Currently, ninety-seven state preserves protect about 10,795 acres. Slightly more than half are owned by the state. The remainder are owned by private parties, conservation organizations, or other public entities. Most state preserves protect significant concentrations of native plant and animal species, rare or endangered species, important geological formations, or some combination thereof. Primary responsibility for historic preservation has been delegated to the Department of Cultural Affairs through the State Historical Society of Iowa. However, many archaeological sites and a few historic sites are designated as state preserves. Forty preserves are featured in this section; five more are included with the state parks and recreation areas.

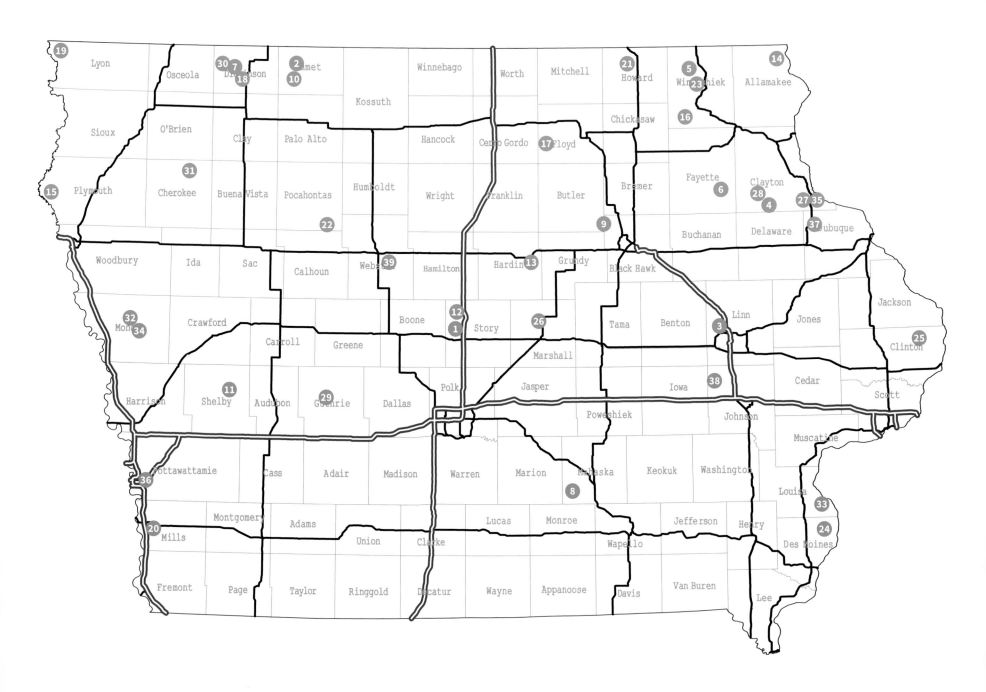

# State Preserves

1 Ames High Prairie State Preserve
2 Anderson Prairie State Preserve
3 Behrens Ponds and Woodland State Preserve
4 Bixby State Preserve
5 Bluffton Fir Stand State Preserve
6 Brush Creek Canyon State Preserve
7 Cayler Prairie State Preserve
8 Cedar Bluffs Natural Area and State Preserve
9 Cedar Hills Sand Prairie State Preserve
10 Cheever Lake State Preserve
11 Dinesen Prairie State Preserve
12 Doolittle Prairie State Preserve
13 Fallen Rock State Preserve

14 Fish Farm Mounds State Preserve
15 Five Ridge Prairie State Preserve
16 Fort Atkinson State Preserve | Saint James Lutheran Church State Preserve
17 Fossil and Prairie Park State Preserve
18 Freda Haffner Kettlehole State Preserve
19 Gitchie Manitou State Preserve
20 Glenwood Archaeological State Preserve
21 Hayden Prairie State Preserve
22 Kalsow Prairie State Preserve
23 Malanaphy Springs State Preserve
24 Malchow Mounds State Preserve
25 Manikowski Prairie State Preserve
26 Marietta Sand Prairie State Preserve
27 Merritt Forest State Preserve

28 Mossy Glen State Preserve
29 Sheeder Prairie State Preserve
30 Silver Lake Fen State Preserve
31 Steele Prairie State Preserve
32 Sylvan Runkel State Preserve
33 Toolesboro Mounds State Preserve
34 Turin Loess Hills State Preserve
35 Turkey River Mounds State Preserve
36 Vincent Bluff State Preserve
37 White Pine Hollow State Preserve
38 Williams Prairie State Preserve
39 Woodman Hollow State Preserve

# Ames High Prairie State Preserve

JOHN PEARSON

The Richard W. Pohl Preserve at Ames High Prairie honors the distinguished professor of botany (1916–1993) at Iowa State University who was an internationally known authority on grasses. This 27-acre remnant of native tallgrass prairie sits in an unlikely spot: nestled between an urban high school and suburban residential neighborhoods.

Iowa State faculty had been aware of this prairie remnant for some time, having made an unsuccessful effort in the late 1940s to obtain it for an outdoor classroom. When the Ames High School District began to discuss development plans for the parcel in the early 1960s, the Ames Conservation Council began working within the community to raise awareness about the site's importance. As a result, in 1970, the residents of Ames passed a formal ballot measure to lease the parcel to the Iowa Chapter of The Nature Conservancy.

Since 1970, the Iowa TNC has managed the preserve, assisted by the Friends of Ames High Prairie, Ames High and Iowa State students, and summer interns. In 1997, it was dedicated as a biological state preserve. Approximately 330 native vascular plant species have been identified in the preserve, and more than a hundred species of birds have been observed here.

# Anderson Prairie State Preserve

LARRY STONE

Anderson Prairie's undulating landscape supports diverse tallgrass prairie communities: dry hilltops, meadows, potholes, and marshlands. More than two hundred native plant species have been identified here. Something is in bloom throughout the growing seasons, from the bell-shaped eastern pasqueflowers of spring to the asters and goldenrods of fall. Butterflies abound, and clusters of monarchs rest in trees during their late summer migration. Bordered by the West Fork of the Des Moines River on the north, the preserve's terrain typifies the gravelly knobs and kettle depressions of the Altamont end moraine, a prominent glacial feature of the Des Moines Lobe landscape.

This area was one of about two dozen native prairie remnants that botanist and prairie ecologist Ada Hayden recommended for protection in the mid-1940s. It is named for the landowner, William Anderson, who sold the 200-acre tract to the state in 1980. In 1984, it was dedicated as a biological and geological state preserve. Although Anderson Prairie is modest in size, it is buffered by a state wildlife management area on the east and two more public areas—Crim Savanna and Ringham Habitat—on the north. Hunting is permitted during open seasons.

# Behrens Ponds and Woodland State Preserve

LARRY STONE

Although small in size, Behrens Ponds and Woodland hosts a remarkable variety of plant and animal communities. Located on the gently rolling Iowan Surface landscape just east of the Cedar River valley in Linn County, the 29-acre preserve features several exceptionally clear natural ponds surrounded by marshy grasslands, oak woodlands, and upland sand prairies. The ponds and surrounding woodlands provide habitat for seventeen species of reptiles and amphibians, including the blue-spotted salamander, which is native to the Great Lakes states, northeastern United States, and parts of Canada but rare in Iowa. A 2001 study identified 348 vascular plant species in the preserve.

Karl W. Behrens donated the property to The Nature Conservancy, Iowa Chapter, in 1977. It was dedicated as a biological state preserve in 1982. Faculty and students at Coe College in Cedar Rapids use the preserve for scientific research and educational field studies.

# Bixby State Preserve

BRIAN GIBBS

In 1926, residents of nearby Edgewood petitioned the Iowa State Board of Conservation to acquire a 69-acre tract once owned by R. J. Bixby, a local businessman and state legislator. It had long been used for picnicking, hiking, trout fishing, and exploring a well-known ice cave. From 1926 to 1979, it was known as Bixby State Park. After the Iowa Conservation Commission purchased an adjoining parcel in 1978, expanding the park to 184 acres, it was rededicated as a biological and geological state preserve in 1979.

Bixby is one of several parks and preserves located along the Silurian Escarpment. Spring-fed Bear Creek flows through a narrow valley 200 feet deep, which is cut into highly fractured and weathered dolomite bedrock. Many interconnecting crevices, especially along the north-facing slopes, enable spring snowmelt, rainfall, and cool, moist air to flow freely downward, forming ice on cold rock surfaces in the spring. The resulting ice cave at Bixby has ice on its rock walls that often lasts well into summer. Bixby's geology supports unique ecological habitats; nearly 400 species of native vascular plants and 105 species of mosses and liverworts have been identified on its heavily wooded rocky slopes, hilltop prairies, and savannas.

# Bluffton Fir Stand State Preserve

CARL KURTZ

In the far reaches of northeast Iowa, near the small town of Bluffton in Winneshiek County, grows a remnant stand of balsam fir, a boreal species typically found much farther north. It is the largest population of balsam fir in Iowa and a reminder that boreal forests once covered much of the state. Natural features along a bend in the Upper Iowa River provide the cool, moist, sheltered conditions these trees need to thrive. Rugged bluffs of Ordovician age limestone rise up nearly 140 feet on the south side of the river. The bluffs are heavily forested, with fir concentrated on the steep, north-facing inclines of the lower slopes. An understory of Canada yew covers the forest floor, and red oaks, sugar maples, and basswood dominate the upper slopes.

Although the fir stand is its central feature, this 94-acre preserve holds a rich mix of plant life. A dry prairie on a steep, rocky, south-facing slope abounds with grasses and wildflowers. In all, more than 350 species of native vascular plants have been recorded in the preserve, which is part of a larger wildlife management area. It was dedicated as a biological and geological state preserve in 1969.

# Brush Creek Canyon State Preserve

CARL KURTZ

The Silurian Escarpment, prominent bluffs of Silurian age dolomite that wind from central Fayette County to southeastern Jackson County, defines a sharp geological boundary in Iowa. The bluff line is frequently interrupted by small narrow gorges and steep ravines, presenting a scenic landscape that geologist Samuel Calvin called the Switzerland of Iowa.

The landscape is particularly dramatic in Brush Creek Canyon, located about 2 miles north of a small town once called Brush Creek but now known as Arlington in southeastern Fayette County. In 1936, residents of Arlington and the surrounding area raised funds to help purchase 150 acres for a state park. In 1941, the Iowa Conservation Commission reclassified the park as a state forest. New botanical studies led to the dedication of Brush Creek Canyon as a biological and geological state preserve in 1968.

Rugged topography creates a variety of habitats that support 351 native vascular plant species, from a dense bottomland forest along Brush Creek in the canyon to a prairie-like patch on top of a large dolomite block in the center of the preserve. More than 75 species of birds have been observed in the preserve, now 217 acres in size.

# Cayler Prairie State Preserve

CARL KURTZ

Botanist and prairie ecologist Ada Hayden examined this 160-acre remnant of native tallgrass prairie in the mid-1940s, at which time it was being used as a hayfield and pasture. She recommended that it be preserved, and in 1958 the Cayler family, who had owned the property since the 1860s, sold it to the Iowa Conservation Commission for this purpose. Located in Dickinson County on the western edge of the last glacier to push into Iowa, about 15,000 years ago, the preserve's hummocky terrain is characteristic of the gravelly ridges and marshy potholes left when the glacial ice stagnated and melted about 12,000 years ago. The preserve is teeming with wildlife, and about 220 native plant species have been identified here.

Faculty and students from nearby Iowa Lakeside Laboratory conduct research on the preserve during the summer months. In 1965 the National Park Service designated Cayler Prairie as a National Natural Landmark, and in 1971 it was dedicated as a biological and geological state preserve. In recent decades, the Iowa Department of Natural Resources has acquired bufferlands, and the Cayler Prairie Complex Wildlife Management Area now protects more than 3,000 acres.

# Cedar Bluffs Natural Area and State Preserve

LARRY STONE

The Mahaska County Conservation Board, in partnership with the Iowa Natural Heritage Foundation, acquired this 225-acre tract of land in 1990 from the Newell Roth estate, although it had been identified as a potential state park as early as 1919. In 1997, it was dedicated as a biological, geological, and archaeological state preserve.

The bluffs define the course of Cedar Creek, which flows into the Des Moines River. This outcropping of reddish sandstone, which rises more than a hundred feet, offers a sweeping view of the Des Moines River valley; it is one of the best exposures of Cherokee Group sandstone in southern Iowa. The Lacey

Memorial Nature Trail honors conservation advocate John F. Lacey, who grew up on a nearby farm. From the bluffs, this loop trail becomes a long stairway that descends the picturesque sandstone outcrops, winds along the creek, then ascends back to the bluffs. Several archaeological sites provide evidence of human use for at least 8,000 years.

The preserve provides habitat for several species of bats, and bald eagles roost in protected areas. More than three hundred plant species have been recorded here, including many ferns, as well as nearly two dozen species of mushrooms.

BRIAN GIBBS

# Cedar Hills Sand Prairie State Preserve

This remnant prairie was more or less discovered by botanists in 1969 as an uncultivated spot on private property northwest of Cedar Falls in Black Hawk County. The University of Northern Iowa Biological Preserves System began managing the site, which the Iowa Chapter of The Nature Conservancy then acquired in 1985 from the Wayne Mark family. That same year, about half of the 80-acre tract was dedicated as a biological and geological state preserve. The Black Hawk County Conservation Board has managed the preserve since 2016 and will assume ownership in 2020.

Cedar Hills Sand Prairie sits on a broad divide mantled with windblown sand deposits between the West Fork of the Cedar River and Beaver Creek. Although it is small, the 36-acre preserve contains a variety of habitats that together support 258 native vascular plant species. A dry sand prairie among the upland ridges transitions to a sedge meadow in a large swale in the northeastern area. A small fen is located within the sedge meadow. Small marshes occupy the southwestern corner of the preserve. More than 50 species of birds, 50 species of butterflies, and several species of small mammals have been recorded here.

207

# Cheever Lake State Preserve

DON POGGENSEE

Until the twentieth century, Cheever Lake in Emmet County was part of an extensive complex of glacial lakes and wetlands common to the Des Moines Lobe region. These waters were created 15,000 to 12,000 years ago during melting phases of the last glacial advance into Iowa. The state of Iowa sold many of its shallow natural lakes and wetlands to be drained for farmland, which almost happened to this one. As of 1905, Cheever Lake was designated for sale and drainage, but for some reason it remained in the public domain and in 1921 came under the jurisdiction of the Iowa Conservation Commission. In 1978, it was dedicated as a biological and geological state preserve.

Cheever Lake is an outstanding example of the pothole marshes that covered much of north-central Iowa before pioneer settlement. The 367-acre preserve also serves as a benchmark for water quality. About ninety wetland plant species grow here, including wild rice and water lilies. The abundant plant life keeps the water exceptionally clear and provides habitat for mink, beaver, muskrat, and many species of frogs and birds. Much of the lake is buffered by the Cheever Lake Wildlife Management Area.

# Dinesen Prairie State Preserve

DON POGGENSEE

When Dinesen Prairie was dedicated as a biological state preserve in 1977, landowner Derald Dinesen told reporters that something akin to "instinct" had driven him to "set aside" this 20-acre remnant of native prairie when, in 1943, he bought his farm northeast of Harlan in Shelby County. He was all of twenty-five at that time. Prairie preservation was still just the dream of a few academic scientists, yet this young farmer—struck by the beauty of native prairie—realized that nearly all of it had been converted to farms, towns, and cities.

The preserve's rolling terrain is typical of southern Iowa, a region of old glacial plains now well drained and carved by modern streams. More than a hundred native vascular plant species grow here. Tall grasses such as porcupinegrass, prairie horsetail, sideoats grama, and Indiangrass can be seen year-round, with an abundance of flowering plants from spring through fall.

When Dinesen died in 1983, his ashes were interred on the prairie, as he wished. A gravestone on top of the hill marks his spot. The Shelby County Conservation Board owns and manages the preserve.

# Doolittle Prairie State Preserve

KEN FORMANEK

Doolittle Prairie is an excellent example of the prairie potholes left in north-central Iowa when the Des Moines Lobe glacial ice was stagnant and slowly melting away 12,000 years ago. Shallow links between some of these wetlands mark the route taken by a meltwater stream.

Named for William and Fidelia Doolittle, settlers who acquired the land in 1855, the preserve contains a 15-acre remnant of native tallgrass prairie (the northernmost area) that has never been plowed or grazed. Another 11 acres, as well as 16 acres adjoining the state preserve on the south, are reconstructed prairie. The state acquired the 26-acre northern tract, also known as the Plover Tract, in 1979 from the Doolittle family and dedicated it as a biological and geological state preserve in 1980. In 1982, the Story County Conservation Board purchased the 16-acre southern tract, known as the Matheason Tract, with the help of the Iowa Natural Heritage Foundation. Both tracts are managed by the conservation board as one unit.

Potholes scattered throughout both units retain water for varying lengths of time, depending on weather conditions. More than 220 species of native plants thrive here, providing habitat for an abundance of birds, butterflies, and mammals.

# Fallen Rock State Preserve

The Hardin County Conservation Board manages more than 4,000 acres of natural areas, parks, and campgrounds, including Fallen Rock State Preserve. Many of these areas are located along the Iowa River Greenbelt, a 42-mile corridor of forested land that edges the river through Hardin County. In 1974, Hardin County purchased the Fallen Rock area, and it was dedicated as a biological and geological state preserve in 1978. Tower Rock County Park borders the preserve on the east, and Fallen Rock Wildlife Area begins at the southwest corner of the preserve.

Within this surprisingly scenic terrain for central Iowa, the Iowa River has carved deeply enough to expose nearly vertical bluffs of Pennsylvanian age sandstone. The preserve is heavily forested, with occasional small meadows, and supports more than three hundred native vascular plant species. Red oaks dominate the forested slopes along the river, with a few white pines on the sandstone bluffs. A rich variety of wildflowers carpets both woodlands and clearings. More than sixty bird species have been recorded here, and because the Iowa River is a flyway for raptors, the preserve is a good place for spotting bald eagles and a variety of hawks during spring and fall migrations.

CARL KURTZ

# Fish Farm Mounds State Preserve

BRIAN GIBBS

Fish Farm Mounds is named for the Fish family, who in 1935 donated to the state a 3-acre parcel that once contained thirty conical prehistoric burial mounds, about half of which are still visible. These mounds were first recorded in the late 1880s.

Archaeological investigations have established that at least some of the mounds are of Middle Woodland age (200 BC–AD 400), and it is likely that people continued to bury and commemorate the dead at this site through the Late Woodland period (AD 400–1250).

The mounds are located in the northeast corner of Allamakee County on an alluvial terrace of sandy sediments deposited when the Mississippi River floodplain was about a hundred feet higher than it is now because of melting glaciers upstream. Erosional downcutting over the past 10,000 years left this remnant of the former floodplain partially protected in a small side valley. The site is sheltered by impressive 300-foot bluffs of Cambrian age sandstone.

Fish Farm Mounds was dedicated as an archaeological state preserve in 1968. Although the preserve encompasses only the mounds, the surrounding picturesque landscape lies within the 912-acre Fish Farm Mounds Wildlife Management Area.

# Five Ridge Prairie State Preserve

DON POGGENSEE

Five Ridge Prairie, one of the largest state preserves in Iowa at 790 acres, is so named for the five prominent northwest-to-southeast-trending ridges of wind-deposited loess that run through the preserve. Situated at the northern end of the scenic Loess Hills region in western Iowa, this preserve displays characteristic peaks and saddles along narrow grass-covered ridges that separate deep wooded valleys. Little bluestem and sideoats grama dominate the drier ridgetops and southwest-facing slopes. Bur oaks are the dominant species in the less exposed wooded valleys.

The Loess Hills region is where the eastern tallgrass prairie transitions to the mixed grasses of the Great Plains. Of the nearly two hundred plant species that have been identified in the preserve, approximately twenty-five are more typical of the drier plains to the west. Wildlife diversity is also high, with at least eighty-nine species of birds, forty-nine butterflies, and twenty mammals.

The Plymouth County Conservation Board owns and manages Five Ridge Prairie, which was purchased from private owners in 1981 with assistance from the Iowa Chapter of The Nature Conservancy and the Iowa Department of Natural Resources. Dedicated in 1986 as a biological and geological state preserve, it is on the Loess Hills National Scenic Byway.

# Fort Atkinson State Preserve | Saint James Lutheran Church State Preserve

Fort Atkinson State Preserve holds the remains of a military post established by the U.S. government in 1840 as part of the long process of relentlessly relocating Native Americans at the same time that Euro-American settlers were pushing westward. It was named for General Henry Atkinson, the army officer in charge of Ho-Chunk (Winnebago) resettlement. Saint James Lutheran Church State Preserve, located about .2 mile northwest of the fort, contains the ruins of a stone church. Both preserves are associated with the early history of the town of Fort Atkinson.

When the federal government sold the abandoned fort in 1855, the purchasers platted the town on former fort land. Decades later, in 1921, at the urging of town residents, the state purchased 5 acres containing the fort buildings and foundations for a state park. In 1968, the site was redesignated and dedicated as a historical, archaeological, and geological state preserve and, in 2015, it was listed on the National Register of Historic Places. In 1970, Saint Peter's Lutheran Church of Eldorado gave the Saint James Lutheran Church property to the state. This one-acre site was dedicated as a historical state preserve the same year.

Directly west of the fort is a quarry of Ordovician age limestone, which furnished stone for the fort as well as the church. The fort, which was used until January 1849, comprised twenty-four buildings and a central parade ground inside a wooden picket stockade wall. Fourteen additional buildings were located outside the stockade. When the state acquired the property in 1921, only three buildings remained

JOHN PEARSON

reasonably intact. Several all-weather panels interpret the history of the buildings, the fort's purpose, and fort life. Since 1977, military reenactors, buckskinners, Native Americans, and craftspeople have gathered here in late September for the Fort Atkinson Rendezvous.

The limestone church was constructed by the First Congregational Church Society of Fort Atkinson. Its precise date of construction—perhaps before 1866— has not been determined, but the building was sold to the German Evangelical Lutheran Saint James Church Society in 1871. A small cemetery associated with the church contains gravestones dated as early as 1874. Gravestone inscriptions in three languages—English, German, and French—indicate the native languages of the town's pioneer settlers.

215

# Fossil and Prairie Park State Preserve

JOHN HILDEBRAND

In 1990, the Floyd County Conservation Board purchased the Rockford Brick and Tile property, where shale had been mined from the early 1880s to 1970, to create a nature park where visitors could hunt for fossils. Geologists had been visiting this site since the 1860s, when information about its significant fossils first appeared in the geological literature. Fossil and Prairie Park quickly became a popular destination. As its popularity grew, so too did a broader awareness of its scientific significance. In 2006, 290 acres of the park were dedicated as a biological, geological, and historical state preserve.

The site, which sprawls west of the floodplain of the Winnebago River, includes steep slopes, numerous gullies, and pits that now hold pools of mineralized water. The exposures of soft shale and limestone belong to the Devonian age. They are rich with well-preserved fossils of marine organisms that inhabited shallow seas 375 million years ago. The preserve also contains more than 55 acres of native prairie. Three of the historic beehive kilns remain.

A visitor center, open May through September, contains a variety of exhibits that connect the geological, biological, and historical components of the park.

# Freda Haffner Kettlehole State Preserve

LARRY STONE

With a bequest from conservationist Freda Haffner of Burlington, Iowa, the Iowa Chapter of The Nature Conservancy purchased the Big Kettle near West Lake Okoboji in 1972. This geological feature, also known as Arend's Kettle Hole, is just what its name implies: a very large bowl-shaped depression created when a giant block of glacial ice lodged along the edge of the Little Sioux River valley and slowly melted in place. It is the largest glacial kettle in Iowa, measuring about 500 feet in diameter and about 30 feet in depth. The 110-acre site was renamed Freda Haffner Kettlehole when it was dedicated as a biological and geological state preserve in 1976.

Nearly 250 species of native vascular plants in diverse prairie communities thrive here, ranging from a wetland in the center of the depression to tallgrass prairie on the slopes to dry prairie on the gravelly rim. In the mid-1940s, botanist and prairie ecologist Ada Hayden included the kettle and its associated prairies on her list of proposed prairie preserves. In the summer, faculty and students from nearby Iowa Lakeside Laboratory use the preserve as an outdoor classroom.

217

# Gitchie Manitou State Preserve

In Algonquian languages, Gitchie Manitou means "great spirit," and terms related to Gitchie Manitou occur in other Amerindian languages. Henry Wadsworth Longfellow popularized the name in his poem *Hiawatha*, which was probably the inspiration for naming this particular place.

Gitchie Manitou also suggests ancientness, and in this respect the preserve is aptly named. Its pink to reddish outcroppings of Sioux Quartzite are the oldest exposed bedrock in Iowa, formed 1.6 billion years ago. These outcrops belong to a ridge of quartzite that runs, roughly, from Pierre, South Dakota, to New Ulm in southwestern Minnesota. American Indian peoples probably gathered stone here, although the quarry site in the preserve, now filled with water and called Jasper Pool, dates from the late nineteenth century.

The state of Iowa purchased the initial 47.5 acres in 1916 for use as a quarry but transferred the site to the Iowa State Board of Conservation in 1926. First designated as a state park, Gitchie Manitou was reclassified as a historical and archaeological area in 1941 and dedicated as a geological, archaeological, historical, and biological state preserve in 1969.

Seventeen low conical burial mounds are located in the preserve's southern area near the Big Sioux River. A recent archaeological study concluded that they belong to the Woodland period (800 BC–AD 1250). The preserve is now in the study area for a potential state park associated with nearby Blood Run National Historic Landmark, an extensive archaeological complex occupied for 8,500 years by numerous prehistoric groups, and Good Earth State Park at Blood Run in South Dakota. Of more recent

CARL KURTZ

vintage are the ruins of a picnic shelter built of Sioux Quartzite in the 1930s as well as the foundations of the Gibraltar post office, part of a short-lived nineteenth-century community, both located in the northern area.

Botanist Bohumil Shimek studied the flora of this area as early as 1898. More recent surveys have recorded 285 native vascular plant species in the 91-acre preserve. A native prairie community grows amid the quartzite outcroppings. Woodlands and wetlands surround Jasper Pool. Former fields in the southern area are now covered with a successional grassland community.

WILLIAM E. WHITTAKER

# Glenwood Archaeological State Preserve

Archaeologist Charles Keyes first applied the name Glenwood Culture to the large concentration of archaeological sites near the Mills County seat of Glenwood. This area around the confluence of the Platte and Missouri Rivers was home to Amerindian peoples who lived in earth lodge dwellings. Although the name Glenwood Culture is still used, archaeologists now label this culture group the Nebraska Culture, a phase of the larger Central Plains tradition. The Nebraska phase refers to ancestors of Pawnee and Arikara who lived along the Missouri River and the lower reaches of the Platte River in Nebraska and around present-day Glenwood from 1200 to 1350. Their square to rectangular semisubterranean lodges and associated artifacts are less well known than the cliff dwellings of the ancestral Pueblo Indians in the Southwest, but both cultures flourished when North American peoples were transitioning from hunting and gathering societies to more settled agricultural lifeways.

Glenwood Archaeological State Preserve was dedicated in 2009 to protect more than 150 recorded archaeological sites, 24 of them likely Nebraska phase earth lodges, a small portion of the more than 500 lodge sites recorded so far in the Glenwood vicinity. This impressive concentration, perhaps the densest concentration in the Midwest and Great Plains, occurs on the east side of the Missouri River across from the mouth of the Platte River.

The 906-acre preserve is located on state-owned land that has been the site of a state-operated mental health institution since 1876 (and from 1866 to 1876 a home for orphans of soldiers who fought in the Civil

WILLIAM E. WHITTAKER

War). In the 1880s, amateur archaeologists began identifying earth lodge sites around Glenwood and collecting artifacts. One of them, Paul Rowe, donated his extensive collection to the Mills County Historical Museum. In 1938, archaeologist Ellison Orr directed extensive professional investigations at Glenwood, aided by residents of the state institution, to map sixty-eight sites and excavate a sample of fifteen lodges. Since then, many investigations have been conducted in connection with graduate studies or as part of environmental studies for flood-control and highway projects.

The preserve is on the Loess Hills National Scenic Byway. In the near future, the Loess Hills Archaeological Interpretive Center will be constructed in the preserve.

221

BRIAN GIBBS

# Hayden Prairie State Preserve

Hayden Prairie pays homage to botanist Ada Hayden, whose name is synonymous with prairie preservation in Iowa. Born in 1884, Hayden grew up on a farm near Ames and went on to spend most of her adult life associated with Iowa State University. She studied botany under Louis Pammel, earning her Ph.D. in 1918. From 1911 until her death in 1950, she taught botany there and continued to collaborate with her mentor. Early in the 1930s, Hayden refocused her attention on prairie plants, which had been the subject of her doctoral dissertation. She gave public presentations on prairie ecology in addition to teaching, conducting floristic research, and, beginning in 1934, serving as curator of the university's herbarium.

In the mid-1940s, Hayden conducted a statewide survey of remnant prairies, which the Iowa Academy of Science published in two reports in 1945 and 1946. By systematically developing a database to inform decisions about land acquisition, she helped launch a modest preservation program that would later inspire a new generation of prairie ecologists. The Iowa Conservation Commission purchased two native prairie tracts in the 1940s: 240 acres in Howard County and 160 acres in Pocahontas County, the latter now known as Kalsow Prairie State Preserve. After Hayden's death, the ICC named the Howard County tract in her honor. In 1968, Hayden Prairie was dedicated as a biological state preserve.

This remnant of black soil prairie, once the most extensive prairie type in Iowa, escaped the plow because it was owned by wealthy easterners who had no interest in farming. It is situated on gently

JOHN PEARSON

rolling terrain where upland and wetland prairie communities intermingle. Big bluestem, Indiangrass, and prairie dropseed dominate the uplands; bluejoint grass, cordgrass, and sedges dominate the wetlands. Many wildflower species bloom here, but Hayden Prairie is especially known for its springtime displays of shooting stars. Surveys have found 220 native plant species here, along with 46 bird species and more than 20 butterfly species. Glacial erratics lie scattered about. In 1965, the National Park Service designated Hayden Prairie as a National Natural Landmark.

# Kalsow Prairie State Preserve

LARRY STONE

Botanist and prairie ecologist Ada Hayden recommended Kalsow Prairie for preservation in the mid-1940s, and in 1948, the Iowa Conservation Commission purchased 160 acres from the Rudolph Kalsow family, one of the pioneer families in Pocahontas County. This quarter section had been used as a hayfield and pasture but never plowed. In 1968, it was dedicated as a biological state preserve.

The terrain is typical of the poorly drained prairie pothole landscape created by the Des Moines Lobe glacier when it stalled, then slowly melted, 12,000 years ago. Although the land appears to be nearly flat, a complex of fourteen potholes scattered across the preserve supports several species of wetland grasses. More than 250 plant species have been recorded here, along with an abundance of birds, amphibians, small mammals, and butterflies. A geological rarity known as the Manson Meteorite Impact Crater lies unseen beneath the surface, buried by much younger glacial deposits. The crater, which measures about 24 miles in diameter, was created when an asteroid or the nucleus of a comet struck the earth about 74 million years ago. One of the largest known impact craters in North America, it was discovered by water-well drillers.

# Malanaphy Springs State Preserve

LARRY STONE

The central feature of this preserve along the Upper Iowa River is a beautiful series of cascading falls that descend from a spring high above in a crevice of Ordovician age dolomite, tumble over a porous lime deposit called tufa, and end in a 10-foot waterfall at the river's edge. Malanaphy Springs, so-named for an early landowner, is a favorite stopping place for river paddlers.

In 1947, newspaper publisher Fred Biermann of Decorah donated the springs to the state. Biermann also served as Iowa's representative from the Fourth Congressional District from 1933 to 1939. His donation helped the state acquire additional land along both sides of the river, which was managed as a wildlife area until 1994, when the unit was designated as a state preserve for its outstanding geological and biological qualities.

The cliffs and rocky slopes of this 64-acre preserve support a remarkable diversity of plant and animal life. More than three hundred vascular plant species occur here as well as many species of land snails and neotropical migrant birds.

# Malchow Mounds State Preserve

WILLIAM E. WHITTAKER

This concentration of prehistoric burial mounds, approximately sixty in number, is one of the largest mound groups in Iowa. Conical and linear in shape, the mounds are asymmetrically crowded into a small area covering approximately 6 acres. When archaeologist Ellison Orr mapped the mounds in 1934, the land was owned by Lewis H. Malchow. A later landowner, Charles Poisel, donated the parcel to the state in 1974, but the name Malchow Mounds was retained when the site was dedicated as an archaeological state preserve in 1978.

The Malchow Mounds are located 13 miles north of Burlington on a loess-covered bluff of Illinoian age glacial drift that overlooks the broad Mississippi River valley. The precise age of the mounds is unknown, but the few artifacts recovered from archaeological investigations indicate a Woodland period (800 BC–AD 1250) age. Nearby are large sites that date to the Middle Woodland (200 BC–AD 400) and Oneota (AD 1250–1700) periods, meaning that the Malchow Mounds may have been in use for millennia.

# Manikowski Prairie State Preserve

LARRY STONE

Manikowski Prairie, 180 acres in size, is located near the small town of Goose Lake in Clinton County. In 1985, the Clinton County Conservation Board, with assistance from the Iowa Natural Heritage Foundation, purchased the initial 40 acres from the Manikowski family. The same year, it was dedicated as a biological and geological state preserve. In 2002, the County Conservation Board and the Natural Heritage Foundation teamed up again to purchase another tract that enlarged the preserve to its present size.

This limestone prairie, a rarity in Iowa, is supported by shallow soils that cover low outcrops of Silurian age dolomite. The outcrops are situated along the eastern edge of a former course taken by the Mississippi River known as the Goose Lake Channel. The Mississippi was temporarily diverted westward through this channel by the Illinoian ice advance into far eastern Iowa nearly 300,000 years ago.

Although the dry upland prairie is dominated by little bluestem and sideoats grama, 138 species of native vascular plants have been recorded here. West of the preserve, the 1,290-acre Goose Lake Wildlife Management Area protects the remaining Goose Lake wetlands.

# Marietta Sand Prairie State Preserve

CARL KURTZ

Sand prairies are among the rarest native habitats that survive in Iowa. In 1983, the Marshall County Conservation Board purchased 17 acres of this remnant sand prairie, funded with a generous donation from Marshall County resident Janet Paterson. Dedicated as a biological and geological state preserve in 1984, it was named Marietta Sand Prairie after the township in which it is located. A large addition of 212 acres in 2006 was made possible through the combined efforts of the Marshall County Conservation Board and the Iowa Natural Heritage Foundation. The total protected area is now 229 acres. In 2005, the Iowa Natural Heritage Foundation also began prairie restoration efforts through annual seed harvests.

Marietta Sand Prairie's unique ecology is tied to its geological origins. The nearby Iowa River and especially Minerva Creek were sources of abundant sand supplied during melting of the Des Moines Lobe ice sheet to the west. During low-flow periods, winds swept up the loose sand and redeposited it across the downwind landscape in drifts as deep as 36 feet here. While the sand prairie is the principal feature, the preserve also includes a sedge meadow and a wetland. These habitats support nearly two hundred plant species.

# Merritt Forest State Preserve

BRIAN GIBBS

Merritt Forest preserves a small tract of old-growth forest south of Guttenberg in Clayton County. Gertrude Merritt of Dubuque donated the tract to the Iowa Conservation Commission in 1968, and it was dedicated as a biological state preserve in 1969.

Naturalists have long been drawn to northeast Iowa because of its rugged landscape. The terrain offers a variety of earth materials, slope angles, and moisture conditions that, in turn, contribute to the greatest biodiversity in the state. Even this small 20-acre preserve, located on a gentle, north-facing incline that slopes toward the Turkey River, contains 192 native vascular plant species, and more than 40 bird species have been observed here. Many species of wildflowers, ferns, mosses, and lichens grow in the preserve, but the main attraction is a stand of old-growth forest dominated by white oak, red oak, sugar maple, and basswood. Some of the oldest and tallest oaks in Iowa are found here. Since 1997, this old forest and its patriarch trees have been monitored with periodic remeasurement of permanent research plots to document long-term changes without human intervention.

# Mossy Glen State Preserve

BRIAN GIBBS

Mossy Glen Creek runs through this 80-acre preserve, which Mildred Hatch donated to the Iowa Conservation Commission in 1978. As a child, Hatch had explored the creek and its wooded valley on her family's farm, and she wished to see the area preserved in memory of her father and uncle, Charles A. and Henry Hesner. It was dedicated as a biological and geological state preserve in 1979.

Mossy Glen is one of several parks and preserves situated along the Silurian Escarpment, prominent winding bluffs of Silurian age dolomite that extend from central Fayette County to southeastern Jackson County. In this particular location, the creek has carved a rugged valley through the dolomite. The presence of underlying impermeable Maquoketa Shale creates springs, which trickle and flow over numerous slumped blocks of dolomite, creating picturesque moss-covered outcroppings framed by steep wooded slopes. Red oak and sugar maple dominate a mature forest with a heavy understory of ironwood, witch hazel, leatherwood, dogwood, bladdernut, and Canada yew. More than three hundred species of vascular plants have been found in the preserve, including many ferns, which thrive in this cool, moist habitat. About sixty species of birds have been observed here.

# Sheeder Prairie State Preserve

BRIAN GIBBS

This 25-acre remnant of native tallgrass prairie takes its name from its last private landowners, Oscar and Clara Sheeder, the son and daughter-in-law of a Guthrie County homesteader. The Sheeder family, who had owned the land for nearly a century, cut hay annually and periodically burned this area of their farm. The rolling terrain of the preserve and surrounding area is characteristic of the Southern Iowa Drift Plain, the predominant landscape of southern Iowa.

Sheeder Prairie was dedicated as a biological state preserve in 1968. More than two hundred species of grasses, wildflowers, and woody vegetation thrive here. During the late spring and summer months, the preserve is teeming with birds. More than sixty species have been recorded, with about twenty-five species nesting here on a regular basis.

# Silver Lake Fen State Preserve

RON JOHNSON

Silver Lake Fen, on the southwestern shore of Silver Lake in Dickinson County, is one of the most mineralized and biologically rich fens in the state. But what is a fen? It is a type of wetland continuously fed by groundwater that slowly seeps to the land surface. Fens usually occur along gentle hillsides in glaciated regions, where mineral-rich groundwater collects between a porous sandy upper layer and a dense clayey lower layer, which halts the water's downward flow. Gravity or sometimes artesian pressure causes the water to move to the land surface at just the right pace to enable decomposing plant material to accumulate, forming peat. The peat deposit creates a special habitat for an unusual community of plants.

Silver Lake Fen is actually a complex of three separate fens. More than a hundred plant species have been identified here, some of them quite rare in Iowa. Purchased by the state in the early 1940s, this 10-acre site was dedicated as a biological and geological state preserve in 1972. Many Iowa botanists have studied the fen, and classes from Iowa Lakeside Laboratory often visit it.

# Steele Prairie State Preserve

DON POGGENSEE

In the mid-1940s, botanist and prairie ecologist Ada Hayden proposed that the state take measures to preserve 320 acres of native tallgrass prairie in Cherokee County, then identified as the Harrison Steele Prairie. The opportunity came in 1986, when The Nature Conservancy and the Iowa Department of Natural Resources jointly purchased 200 acres, in two separate tracts, from the Steele family. Prairie hay had been harvested from these areas, but they had escaped the plow. In 1987 it was dedicated as a biological state preserve. It is named for T. H. Steele, who founded Steele State Bank in Cherokee in 1874. Harrison Steele, his son, served as bank president from 1928 to 1951,

then stepped down to run Steele, Inc., which managed farms and other real estate.

The preserve's rolling terrain supports 222 native plant species that flourish in dry and wet prairie communities. Big bluestem, prairie dropseed, and porcupine grass dominate the slopes and drier uplands. Sedges, bluejoint grass, and prairie cordgrass dominate the drainageways. Diverse wildflower species bloom throughout the spring and summer.

# Sylvan Runkel State Preserve

Sylvan Runkel State Preserve honors one of Iowa's foremost conservationists. After earning a bachelor's degree in forestry from Iowa State University, Sy Runkel worked as a forester in various capacities before being appointed superintendent of the first Civilian Conservation Corps camp organized in Iowa, at Albia. He then joined the Soil Conservation Service in 1934. His career as a forester-conservationist spanned almost four decades, with time out to serve as a glider pilot in the U.S. Army Air Corps during World War II. In 1952, he became the Soil Conservation Service biologist for the state of Iowa, and he served on the State Preserves Advisory Board from 1969 to 1979.

When Runkel retired in 1972, he began a second career as a public figure, coauthoring five books on midwestern wildflowers and receiving many honors for his service to conservation organizations. He was particularly effective as a popular educator. In addition to helping develop a natural history series for Iowa Public Television, he led field trips for many years at the Loess Hills Prairie Seminar, an annual event then sponsored by the Western Hills Area Education Agency. A year after his death in 1995, this 550-acre portion of the Loess Hills Wildlife Management Area was dedicated as a biological and geological state preserve in his name.

The dramatic Loess Hills topography, with its narrow ridge crests and distinctive peaks and saddles, displays all its natural beauty here. More than two hundred plant species, one hundred bird species, and fifty-six butterfly species have been observed in the general area. The 12-mile Loess

JOHN PEARSON

Hills loop trail, which begins in the adjoining Loess Hills Wildlife Management Area, travels through the preserve. Designated as part of the Loess Hills National Natural Landmark site by the National Park Service in 1986, the preserve is on the Loess Hills National Scenic Byway.

# Toolesboro Mounds State Preserve

The Toolesboro Mounds, remnants of a much larger complex, are situated on a high narrow divide above the confluence of the Iowa and Mississippi Rivers. Based on surviving artifacts and excavation records, archaeologists have associated the mounds with a regional group known as the Havana tradition (200 BC–AD 400) who participated in the extensive trade networks of the Hopewell tradition, which flourished along northeastern and midwestern rivers.

In the 1930s, the Iowa Archeological Society and the State Historical Society of Iowa called on the state to preserve the remaining mounds, but nothing happened until 1963, when the George H. Mosier family donated two of the mounds to the state. The other five mounds were acquired in 1976. The mound group was designated as a National Historic Landmark and listed on the National Register of Historic Places in 1966, and it was dedicated as an archaeological state preserve in 1981. A museum administered by the State Historical Society of Iowa is open during summer months. The 5-acre site is managed by the Louisa County Conservation Board.

# Turin Loess Hills State Preserve

In the heart of the hills, this preserve, together with the Turin Prairie Addition and the Loess Hills Wildlife Management Area, protects nearly 5,400 acres of Loess Hills landscape. In turn, these three areas are part of the 10,454-acre Loess Hills National Natural Landmark site, a mix of state and privately owned lands designated by the National Park Service in 1986 as presenting the best example of this unusual terrain and its associated ecology.

Turin Loess Hills' 220 acres, dedicated as a biological and geological state preserve in 1978, offer dramatic views of steeply pitched west-facing hillsides contrasting with the wide, flat Missouri River valley. Many of the plants are more typical of the Great Plains than the tallgrass prairie. Of the more than seven hundred species found throughout the Loess Hills, some, such as yucca and sand lily, occur only in this region of Iowa.

DON POGGENSEE

# Turkey River Mounds State Preserve

Turkey River Mounds State Preserve protects a large group of prehistoric mounds arrayed along a high narrow ridge south of Guttenberg in Clayton County. The site has long been of scientific interest. Archaeologists conducted exploratory surveys in the late nineteenth century, and T. H. Lewis mapped the mounds in 1885. To preserve them, residents of Dubuque purchased a 62-acre tract in 1934 and donated it to the state in 1940. The tract was dedicated as a state preserve in 1968. It is also on the National Register of Historic Places.

The precipitous ridge on which the mounds are situated provides a striking overlook of the confluence of the Turkey and Mississippi Rivers. Nearly vertical bluffs of weathered Ordovician age dolomite rise more than 200 feet above the floodplains. At the summit, forty-three conical, linear, compound, and effigy mounds represent a long period of human use dating from the Late Archaic to the Middle Woodland period (2500 BC–AD 400). About twenty-five of the mounds are still visible. In the 1960s, archaeologist Marshall McKusick excavated some of the burial mounds. His findings revealed unusual burial practices that involved the construction of shallow circular ditches and stone barriers. Scholars have hypothesized that such constructions were intended either to contain ghosts or to shield the dead from supernatural malice.

Nearly 350 native vascular plant species have been recorded in the preserve. The semiforested ridge gives way to prairie openings near the cliff edges. Ferns and lichens grow on the dolomite outcrops. White oak and shagbark hickory dominate the dry, south-facing

JOHN PEARSON

slope beneath the bluffs; sugar maple and basswood dominate the mesic, north-facing slope.

LARRY STONE

239

# Vincent Bluff State Preserve

LARRY STONE

In the mid-1990s, concerned citizens of Council Bluffs organized as the Loess Hills Preservation Society to protect the Loess Hills where this unique landscape nestles into the city's east side. In 2000, the Iowa Natural Heritage Foundation assisted their efforts by purchasing 31 acres from Mildred Vincent (1921–2002), a retired small business owner. In 2001, the city of Council Bluffs took an equally big step by enacting the Loess Hills Preservation Plan to help guide development in the hills that are the city's namesake. The city also purchased Vincent Bluff from the INHF in 2002, funded by grants and private donations.

The Loess Hills Preservation Society, which manages Vincent Bluff under an agreement with the city, purchased an additional 10 acres and sought state preserve status. By the time Vincent Bluff was dedicated as a biological, geological, and scenic state preserve in 2009, the society had helped raise more than $1 million from approximately four hundred individuals, organizations, and foundations. The society had also mobilized more than 10,000 hours of volunteer service to remove fences, invasive species, and dumped materials and then to begin the process of prairie restoration.

# White Pine Hollow State Preserve

BRIAN GIBBS

In 1934, the Dubuque County Conservation Society helped the Iowa State Board of Conservation acquire 80 acres of old-growth white pines. The board designated the tract as a forest preserve. Acquisition of additional lands followed, and the 792-acre preserve was dedicated as a biological and geological state preserve in 1968. At about the same time, the National Park Service designated the area as a National Natural Landmark. The preserve is buffered on the south and northeast by the White Pine Wildlife Management Area, and the 819-acre Ram Hollow Wildlife Management Area is located nearby.

The preserve holds an astounding variety of natural features, plants, and animals. One of the more unusual geological features is a "rock city" in the southeastern portion of the preserve, formed by the haphazard separation of blocks of dolomite that created a maze of narrow pathways. Diverse habitats support 508 native plant species and 117 lichen species. Several species of land snails thrive in the cool, moist air that seeps from bedrock fissures. About 90 species of birds have been observed throughout the preserve as well as 6 species of bats.

# Williams Prairie State Preserve

JOHN PEARSON

Williams Prairie, a 30-acre tract of native prairie located in western Johnson County, came to the attention of botanists from the University of Iowa in the early 1960s. It is named for John Williams, who purchased the land in about 1910 and used it as a hayfield. The Iowa Chapter of The Nature Conservancy acquired the property in 1973, and in 1976 it was dedicated as a biological state preserve. In 2014, TNC deeded the prairie to the Johnson County Conservation Board following a trial management period supported by TNC and the State Preserves Advisory Board. Faculty and students from the University of Iowa, Cornell College, and local high schools conduct field studies and scientific research here, and it is a popular spot for organized nature hikes.

The prairie is situated roughly in the center of an undrained depression within the Iowa River valley. A few dry knolls are located in the eastern and southern areas, but most of the preserve remains wet into the summer months. Dense stands of bluejoint grass and sedges dominate the wetlands, although many species of grasses grow here, and many nesting birds inhabit the preserve. Williams Prairie supports 278 native plant species and is especially known for grand displays of marsh marigolds in late April.

# Woodman Hollow State Preserve

Woodman Hollow has the distinction of being the first state preserve. When the state purchased this 63.5-acre parcel from the Woodman family in 1927, Central States Electric Company was seeking approval to build a hydroelectric dam on the Des Moines River. One proposed location would have flooded the hollow. The Iowa State Board of Conservation and many local residents vigorously opposed the dam at this location, which convinced the state to approve an alternate site. Woodman Hollow was so highly valued for its biodiversity that the Board of Conservation declared it to be "a reserve for the full protection of plant and animal life therein."

After passage of the State Preserves Act in 1965, Woodman Hollow was formally dedicated as a biological, geological, and archaeological state preserve. A rich variety of ferns and mosses grows in the steep narrow ravine of Pennsylvanian age sandstone that is its central feature. Surveys have recorded 534 native vascular plant species and 142 species of mosses, liverworts, and hornworts. Two rock shelters provide evidence of Native American occupation during the Woodland period (800 BC–AD 1250).

CARL KURTZ

# State Forests

In the 1920s, Louis Pammel, chair of the Iowa State Board of Conservation, and Gilmour B. MacDonald, professor of forestry at Iowa State University and deputy state forester under the Iowa Department of Agriculture, shoehorned forestry into state park development. Initially, MacDonald simply supplied the Board of Conservation with nursery stock from Iowa State for planting in state parks. After 1925, the board allowed the university's Forestry Department to use state parks to grow native trees and shrubs to carry out reforestation in the parks.

A cluster of developments in the 1930s made it possible to establish a real forestry program. The 1933 Iowa Twenty-five Year Conservation Plan identified woodlands as a pressing conservation problem. That same year, MacDonald was appointed state director of the federal Emergency Conservation Work program, with authority over all Civilian Conservation Corps camps in Iowa and the funds that came for this program. As a result, many CCC camps in Iowa were, at one time or another, assigned to forestry and soil conservation work. In 1935, when the Iowa legislature merged the Board of Conservation and the Fish and Game Commission into a new agency, the Iowa Conservation Commission, forestry was recognized as a legitimate function of the ICC, and MacDonald was officially designated as state forester.

As the Emergency Conservation Work director and official state forester, MacDonald was thus in a position to establish forest reserves as funds became available. In the early 1930s, he also conducted a forest and wasteland survey that caught the attention of the U.S. National Forest Reservation Commission. This led to the commission's approval, in 1935, to purchase more than 800,000 acres of distressed farmland in southern Iowa for reforestation and the establishment of a national forest. MacDonald also proposed federal purchase of another 800,000 acres in northeast Iowa, the Loess Hills, and elsewhere in Iowa.

Proposals to acquire up to 1.6 million acres for reforestation were far beyond realistic. However, by the early 1940s, the state had purchased more than 11,000 acres of tax-delinquent land in Lucas, Monroe, Lee, Van Buren, Allamakee, and Clayton Counties, and three state forest reserves were established. The U.S Forest Service had purchased another 4,400 acres of distressed, tax-delinquent land in proximity to the two reserves in southeastern Iowa. These state and federal purchases formed the core of Shimek, Stephens, and Yellow River State Forests.

World War II stalled Iowa's forestry program. The Forest Service also abandoned its plan for a national forest in Iowa and eventually transferred federal holdings to the state in the 1960s. However, post–World War II demand for outdoor recreation led to a new source of federal funds—the Land and Water Conservation Fund—for national and state park expansion on a level that rivaled that of the 1930s. Between 1966 and the early 1980s, when funding levels were drastically cut, Iowa received more than $40 million in LWCF grants. Some of the grants were used to purchase land to expand state forests. As funding from the LWCF tapered off, Iowa began to generate new revenue sources for outdoor recreation through a state lottery and then through the Resource Enhancement and Protection program. These three sources have funded land purchases to create the Loess Hills State Forest.

Almost all state forests in Iowa were created by purchasing land rather than setting aside public lands. Thus, they are composed of land units, some quite large and others relatively small. In addition to four major forests—Yellow River, Shimek, Stephens, and Loess Hills—the system includes seven smaller forests. These are Backbone State Forest, adjacent to Backbone State Park in Delaware County; White Pine Hollow State Forest in Dubuque County, most of which was dedicated as a state preserve in 1968; Merritt Forest State Preserve in Clayton County; Holst, Barkley, and Pilot Mound State Forests, all in Boone County; and Gifford State Forest in Pottawattamie County. Together, they total nearly 44,000 acres.

With some exceptions, state forests are managed for multiple benefits: to maintain healthy woodlands, provide wildlife habitat and outdoor recreation opportunities, and produce nursery stock as well as forest products. Some state forests sell lumber and firewood to the public. Hunting is allowed on state forests except near campgrounds. All state forests are open to hiking, fishing, and wildlife watching as well as horseback riding, cross-country skiing, and snowmobiling on designated trails. Merritt Forest and most of White Pine Hollow State Forest are managed as preserves, and Gifford State Forest, a 40-acre tract located within the city limits of Council Bluffs, is managed as a wildlife refuge.

# State Forests

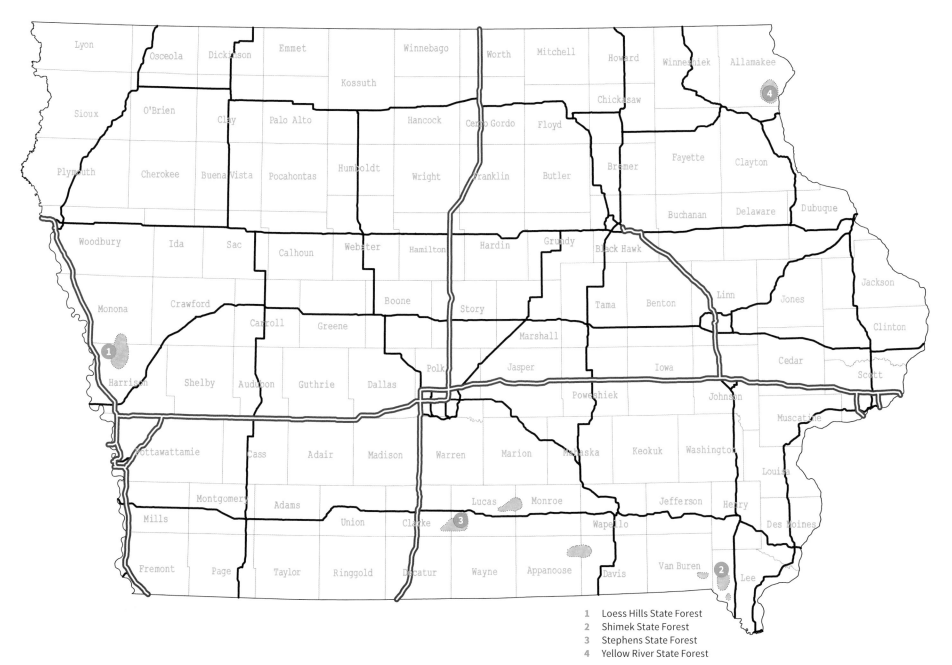

**1** Loess Hills State Forest
**2** Shimek State Forest
**3** Stephens State Forest
**4** Yellow River State Forest

# Loess Hills State Forest

Loess Hills State Forest, initially known as Loess Hills Pioneer State Forest, was the fourth major state forest to be established in Iowa. Land purchases began in 1986, and since then additional land has been purchased incrementally from willing sellers. Today, the forest protects 11,692 acres of the Loess Hills landscape in four separate units: Little Sioux, Preparation Canyon, Pisgah, and Mondamin. These units span two counties, Harrison and Monona, in the middle reach of the Loess Hills. The hills have been called Iowa's fragile giants because they are composed primarily of massive deposits of windblown silt—loess—that is highly susceptible to erosion. The thickest and most widespread of several episodes of loess deposition formed 27,000 to 12,500 years ago when westerly winds carried it from the Missouri River floodplain and deposited it in a band that stretches nearly the length of Iowa's western border. Erosion by streams and gullies then carved valleys into these deposits, producing the region's distinctive steeply ridged terrain.

Although the state forest was established relatively recently, the Loess Hills region has been the target of conservation efforts since the 1930s because the silty soil erodes so easily. Preparation Canyon State Park, adjacent to the Preparation Canyon Forest Unit, was initially called a forest preserve when the Iowa State Board of Conservation acquired it in 1935. The Jones Creek Watershed Project, one of the few Civilian Conservation Corps' soil erosion projects to be carried out on privately owned land, is now part of the Preparation Canyon Unit. Jones Creek Watershed, which includes a small lake, is listed on the National Register of Historic Places.

IOWA TOURISM

Public hunting is allowed throughout the forest, and 38 miles of trails across the four units are open to hiking and cross-country skiing. A universally accessible observation deck in the Preparation Canyon Unit offers a commanding view of the interior of the hills. In 1989, the town of Pisgah donated 3 acres for a forest headquarters. Pisgah is also the site of a visitor center opened in 1999 to interpret the region's natural and cultural history; it was renamed the Brent S. Olson Memorial Visitor Center in 2017 to honor the late area forester. The forest is on the Loess Hills National Scenic Byway.

# Shimek State Forest

Shimek State Forest covers more than 9,400 acres of Lee and Van Buren Counties in far southeastern Iowa. Shimek comprises five units: Croton, Donnellson, Farmington, Keosauqua, and Lick Creek. The first four are named for nearby towns; Lick Creek is named for the stream that flows through it. The first land acquisitions occurred in 1936 when the state began purchasing tax-delinquent lands for reforestation. The Croton Unit is made up of three subunits acquired from the U.S. Forest Service in 1964.

The landscape of Shimek State Forest is characterized by well-drained rolling terrain, with oak and hickory trees covering the uplands and side slopes along the Des Moines River valley. Bottomland hardwoods include elm, cottonwood, hackberry, silver maple, and black walnut trees. About a thousand acres have been planted with conifers. Native prairie grasses and wildflowers occur in the openings.

Initially, the forest was referred to as the Lee and Van Buren State Forest, then as Farmington State Forest. In the 1950s, the name was changed to Shimek State Forest to honor Bohumil Shimek (1861–1937), professor of botany at the University of Iowa and one of many natural scientists in Iowa who were active in the conservation movement. Shimek was a charter member of the Iowa Park and Forestry Association as well as its successor, the Iowa Conservation Association. He served as president of the Iowa Academy of Science in 1904 and 1905 and assisted the Iowa Geological Survey from 1907 to 1929. His knowledge of Iowa's natural history was both broad and deep, and he published many articles on scientific topics and conservation issues.

LORA CONRAD

Hunting and hiking are allowed throughout the forest, although trail conditions vary. The Donnellson, Farmington, and Lick Creek Units, which are roughly contiguous, contain four small fishing lakes, nonmodern campgrounds, and extensive trail systems: 25 miles of hiking trails in the Donnellson and Farmington Units and 27 miles of multiple-use trails for horseback riding, mountain biking, and hiking in the Lick Creek Unit. Members of the Friends of Shimek State Forest help maintain the Lick Creek Unit trails. The Croton Unit, the southernmost unit, has no recreational infrastructure but is known for its excellent bird watching. The Keosauqua Unit, the smallest unit, has 1.4 miles of hiking trails. Additionally, it is situated between Lacey-Keosauqua State Park on the east and Lake Sugema Wildlife Management Area on the west, both of which are well developed for outdoor recreation.

# Stephens State Forest

The 15,500 acres of Stephens State Forest sprawl across parts of five southeastern counties: Clarke, Lucas, Monroe, Appanoose, and Davis. The largest of Iowa's state forests, Stephens comprises seven units: the roughly contiguous Woodburn, Whitebreast, and Lucas Units in Clarke and Lucas Counties; the Cedar Creek, Chariton, and Thousand Acres Units in Lucas and Monroe Counties; and the eleven subunits of the Unionville Unit in Appanoose and Davis Counties. Forest lands are a mix of tax-delinquent tracts purchased by the state in the 1930s, tracts purchased by the U.S. Forest Service and transferred to the state in the 1960s, and tracts purchased more recently from willing sellers.

The landscape is characterized by steeply rolling terrain in an area of the state where Pennsylvanian age coal deposits were once mined. Forested tracts follow the valleys of Whitebreast, North Cedar, and Soap Creeks, drainages carved into the loess-mantled Pre-Illinoian glacial drifts that cover much of southern Iowa. Oaks and hickory trees predominate on the uplands. Elm, cottonwood, hackberry, silver maple, and black walnut trees are found in the bottomlands. Plantations of pine, spruce, black locust, tulip poplar, and other tree species occur throughout the forest, some of them planted by Civilian Conservation Corps crews in the 1930s.

For many years, the forest was known as the Lucas-Monroe Forest. In 1951, the name was changed to Stephens State Forest to honor T. C. Stephens (1876–1948), professor of biology at Morningside College in Sioux City. Stephens was a noted ornithologist and conservationist who championed wildlife conservation in particular. Among his many achievements, he received a gold medal presented by the Permanent

WARREN TERPSTRA

Wild Life Protection Fund for his vigorous efforts to help pass the 1917 Turner Quail Bill, which marked the first time Iowa authorized a multiyear closed season to allow a threatened species time to repopulate. It is thus fitting that Stephens State Forest was designated as a Bird Conservation Area in 2008.

Hiking and hunting are allowed throughout the forest. However, most of the recreational development is located in the Woodburn, Whitebreast, and Lucas Units. The Woodburn Unit has more than 6 miles of backpacking trails and five pack-in campsites. The Whitebreast Unit has two fishing ponds, three equestrian campgrounds, one group campground, and 20 miles of multiple-use trails for horseback riding, mountain biking, and cross-country skiing. The Lucas Unit has two fishing ponds, three campgrounds, and 5 miles of multiple-use trails. The other units do not have any recreational infrastructure, but dirt roads and service lanes provide access for hunting, backcountry hiking, and wildlife watching.

# Yellow River State Forest

Yellow River State Forest covers more than 8,900 acres of scenic rugged terrain in Allamakee County near the Mississippi River. It is composed of six units, the oldest of which, the Yellow River Unit, was purchased in the mid-1930s and named for the river that flows through it. The Paint Creek Unit, the largest unit, lies within the Paint Creek Watershed, which is drained by Little Paint and Big Paint Creeks. The Luster Heights and Waukon Junction Units are also in the Paint Creek Watershed. Luster Heights is named for the previous landowner, Waukon Junction for the hamlet located near its south end. The Paint Rock Unit is named for the American Indian petroglyphs and remnants of rock paintings found on a bluff along the Mississippi River. The Mud Hen Unit, named for the American coot, also called the mud hen, is made up of islands and sloughs in the Mississippi River, surrounded by and for all practical purposes indistinguishable from the Mud Hen Lake Wildlife Management Area.

The chiseled landscape of Yellow River State Forest, except for the Mud Hen Unit, begins with Cambrian age sandstones and Ordovician age dolomites that are exposed in far northeast Iowa. Rivers and streams carved deep valleys through these bedrock layers as their waters tumbled to the Mississippi River, creating steep slopes and high bluffs. Sugar maple, basswood, white ash, and elms predominate on north- and east-facing slopes. Oaks, elms, and hickory thrive on drier south- and west-facing slopes and blufftops. Several plantations of conifers, native hardwoods, and experimental species are located throughout the forest.

Much of the forest consists of former farmland that has been replanted with trees. However, timber harvesting also began in the 1930s, providing construction materials used in developing state parks. Civilian Conservation Corps crews performed this work until the CCC was phased out in the early 1940s. In 1949, the state transferred 1,500 acres of the Yellow River Unit to the National Park Service in order to create Effigy Mounds National Monument. This reduced the size of the forest considerably, but as demand for outdoor recreation began to grow in the 1950s and 1960s, the Iowa Conservation Commission gradually acquired land from willing sellers, expanding the forest to its current size and configuration. Since 1947, a sawmill in the Paint Creek Unit has produced lumber for building construction in state parks. From the early 1960s to 2017, the Luster Heights Unit was also home to the Luster Heights Correctional Facility, a minimum-security camp for fifty to eighty inmates who helped maintain the forest and also held jobs in surrounding communities.

The Paint Creek Unit contains most of the forest's recreational facilities. It has two nonmodern campgrounds, two nonmodern equestrian campgrounds, one camping cabin, five backpacking campsites, several picnic areas, and 6 miles of trout stream stocked from April through October. Hiking trails are maintained at Paint Creek and Luster Heights; designated cross-country ski trails are maintained at Luster Heights. The entire forest is open to hunting on a seasonal basis.

# Further Reading

Many writers, photographers, educators, and artists have documented Iowa's natural world and environmental history. The works listed below are readily available in public libraries, at booksellers, and online.

**The Archaeological Guide to Iowa** *by William E. Whittaker, Lynn M. Alex, and Mary C. De La Garza.* Iowa City: University of Iowa Press, 2015.

**Bedrock Geologic Map of Iowa.** Iowa City: Iowa Geological and Water Survey, Iowa Department of Natural Resources, 2010. Online at https://ir.uiowa.edu/igs_ofm/71/.

**Birds of an Iowa Dooryard** *by Althea R. Sherman, foreword by Marcia Myers Bonta.* Iowa City: University of Iowa Press, 1996.

**The Butterflies of Iowa** *by Dennis W. Schlicht, John C. Downey, and Jeffrey Nekola.* Iowa City: University of Iowa Press, 2007.

**A Country So Full of Game: The Story of Wildlife in Iowa** *by James J. Dinsmore.* Iowa City: University of Iowa Press, 1994.

**Deep Nature: Photographs from Iowa,** *photographs by Linda Scarth and Robert Scarth, essay by John Pearson.* Iowa City: University of Iowa Press, 2009.

**The Emerald Horizon: The History of Nature in Iowa** *by Cornelia F. Mutel.* Iowa City: University of Iowa Press, 2008.

**Enchanted by Prairie,** *photographs by Bill Witt, essay by Osha Gray Davidson.* Iowa City: University of Iowa Press, 2009.

**Forest and Shade Trees of Iowa,** *3d edition, by Peter van der Linden and Donald Farrar.* Iowa City: University of Iowa Press, 2011.

**Fragile Giants: A Natural History of the Loess Hills** *by Cornelia F. Mutel.* Iowa City: University of Iowa Press, 1989.

**Gladys Black: The Legacy of Iowa's Bird Lady** *by Larry A. Stone and Jon W. Stravers.* Elkader: Turkey River Environmental Expressions, 2010.

**Guidebooks to selected state parks from the Geological Society of Iowa and the Iowa Geological Survey.** Online at https://www.iihr.uiowa.edu/igs/guidebooks-around-iowa/.

**The Guide to Iowa's State Preserves** *by Ruth Herzberg and John Pearson.* Iowa City: University of Iowa Press for the Iowa Department of Natural Resources, 2001. Also online at https://www.iowadnr.gov/Places-to-Go/State-Preserves.

**An Illustrated Guide to Iowa Prairie Plants** *by Paul Christiansen and Mark Müller.* Iowa City: University of Iowa Press, 1999.

**The Indians of Iowa** *by Lance Foster.* Iowa City: University of Iowa Press, 2010.

**Iowa: Portrait of the Land** *edited by Jean C. Prior, lead writer Larry A. Stone, illustrations by Mark Müller.* Des Moines: Iowa Department of Natural Resources, 2000.

**Iowa Birdlife** *by Gladys Black, foreword by Dean M. Roosa, introduction by Carl Kurtz.* Iowa City: University of Iowa Press, 1992.

**The Iowa Breeding Bird Atlas** *by Laura Spess Jackson, Carol A. Thompson, and James J. Dinsmore.* Iowa City: University of Iowa Press, 1996.

**Iowa Fish and Fishing** *by James R. Harlan and Everett B. Speaker.* Des Moines: Iowa Department of Natural Resources, 1987.

**Iowa Geology.** Annual issues from the Iowa Geological Survey, 1980 to 2001, contain nontechnical articles about interesting and important aspects of Iowa's geology. Online at https://ir.uiowa.edu/iowageology/.

**The Iowa Lakeside Laboratory: A Century of Discovering the Nature of Nature** *by Michael J. Lannoo.* Iowa City: University of Iowa Press, 2012.

**The Iowa Nature Calendar** *by Jean C. Prior and James Sandrock, illustrations by Claudia McGehee.* Iowa City: University of Iowa Press, 2010.

**Iowa's Geological Past: Three Billion Years of Change** *by Wayne I. Anderson.* Iowa City: University of Iowa Press, 1998.

**Iowa's Natural Heritage** *by Tom Cooper and Nyla Sherburne Hunt.* Des Moines: Iowa Natural Heritage Foundation and the Iowa Academy of Science, 1982.

**Iowa's Wild Places: An Exploration with Carl Kurtz** *by Carl Kurtz.* Ames: Iowa State University Press, 1996.

**Landform Regions of Iowa—2017** (map). Iowa City: Iowa Geological Survey, University of Iowa Hydroscience and Engineering. Online at https://www.iihr.uiowa.edu/igs/landforms-map/.

**Landforms of Iowa** *by Jean C. Prior.* Iowa City: University of Iowa Press, 1991.

**Land of the Fragile Giants: Landscapes, Environments, and Peoples of the Loess Hills** *edited by Cornelia F. Mutel and Mary Swander.* Iowa City: University of Iowa Press, 1994.

**Listen to the Land: Selections from 25 Years of Naturalist Writing in the "Des Moines Register,"** *2d edition, by Larry A. Stone.* Elkader: Turkey River Environmental Expressions, 2004.

**Mammals of Iowa Field Guide** *by Michael Rentz, Vince Evelsizer, Stephanie Shepherd, and Adam Janke.* Ames: Iowa State University Extension and Outreach, 2018.

**A More Beautiful Iowa: Iowa's State Parks System,** *exhibit by Laura Sullivan and others.* Ames: Iowa State University Special Collections and University Archives, 2017. Online at https://exhibits.lib.iastate.edu/iowa-state-parks.

**Mushrooms and Other Fungi of the Midcontinental United States,** *2d edition, by D. M. Huffman, L. H. Tiffany, G. Knaphus, and R. A. Healy.* Iowa City: University of Iowa Press, 2008.

**Okoboji Wetlands: A Lesson in Natural History** *by Michael J. Lannoo.* Iowa City: University of Iowa Press, 1996.

**Oneota Flow: The Upper Iowa River and Its People** *by David Faldet.* Iowa City: University of Iowa Press, 2009.

**Places of Quiet Beauty: Parks, Preserves, and Environmentalism** *by Rebecca Conard.* Iowa City: University of Iowa Press, 1997.

**Pocket guides from the University of Iowa Press.** Guides to look for include birds at your feeder, butterflies, dragonflies and damselflies, fish, frogs and toads, gems and minerals, grasses, moths, mushrooms, orchids, prairie, projectile points, raptors, salamanders, snakes and lizards, trees, turtles, warblers, waterfowl, wetlands, and woodlands.

**A Practical Guide to Prairie Reconstruction,** *2d edition, by Carl Kurtz.* Iowa City: University of Iowa Press, 2013.

**The Raptors of Iowa,** *paintings by James F. Landenberger, essays by Dean M. Roosa, Jon W. Stravers, Bruce Ehresman, and Rich Patterson.* Iowa City: University of Iowa Press, 2013.

**Shrubs and Vines of Iowa** *by Peter van der Linden and Donald Farrar.* Iowa City: University of Iowa Press, 2016.

**Stratigraphic Column of Iowa 2017.** Iowa City: Iowa Geological Survey, University of Iowa Hydroscience and Engineering. Online at https://www.iihr.uiowa.edu/igs/stratigraphic-column/.

**Sylvan T. Runkel: Citizen of the Natural World** *by Larry A. Stone and Jon W. Stravers.* Elkader: Turkey River Environmental Expressions, 2003.

**A Tallgrass Prairie Alphabet** *by Claudia McGehee.* Iowa City: University of Iowa Press, 2004.

**The Tallgrass Prairie Center Guide to Prairie Restoration in the Upper Midwest** *by Daryl Smith, Dave Williams, Greg Houseal, and Kirk Henderson.* Iowa City: University of Iowa Press, 2010.

**A Tallgrass Prairie Reader** *edited by John T. Price.* Iowa City: University of Iowa Press, 2014.

**The Vascular Plants of Iowa: An Annotated Checklist and Natural History** *by Lawrence J. Eilers and Dean M. Roosa.* Iowa City: University of Iowa Press, 1994.

**Where the Sky Began: Land of the Tallgrass Prairie** *by John Madson.* 1982; reprint Iowa City: University of Iowa Press, 2004.

**Wildflowers and Other Plants of Iowa Wetlands,** *2d edition, by Sylvan T. Runkel and Dean M. Roosa.* Iowa City: University of Iowa Press, 2015.

**Wildflowers of Iowa Woodlands,** *2d edition, by Sylvan T. Runkel and Alvin F. Bull.* Iowa City: University of Iowa Press, 2010.

**Wildflowers of the Tallgrass Prairie: The Upper Midwest** *by Sylvan T. Runkel and Dean M. Roosa.* Iowa City: University of Iowa Press, 2010.

**A Woodland Counting Book** *by Claudia McGehee.* Iowa City: University of Iowa Press, 2006.

**A Year of Iowa Nature: Discovering Where We Live** *by Carl Kurtz.* Iowa City: University of Iowa Press, 2014.

# Notes on Contributors

**Rebecca Conard** is professor of history emeritus at Middle Tennessee State University and the former director of the MTSU Public History Program. Her publications include several works on the history of parks and protected areas, most notably *Places of Quiet Beauty: Parks, Preserves, and Environmentalism*, an environmental history of the Iowa state park system. After retiring from teaching in 2016, she returned to her native state of Iowa.

**Angela Corio** holds a degree in landscape architecture from Iowa State University. During her thirty-six-year career as a state park planner with the Iowa Department of Natural Resources, she combined her passion for bringing people outdoors with her love of the Iowa landscape. Her planning efforts included almost all Iowa state park improvements, continuing a tradition of conjoining landscape architecture and park planning that began in Iowa in 1925. Her most notable accomplishments were comprehensive master plans for Iowa's largest recreation areas—Volga and Brushy Creek—as well as redevelopment plans for older parks such as Pikes Peak, Maquoketa Caves, and Viking Lake; recreation-use plans for twenty-five other parks; and the Iowa State Parks Design Guide: Long-Term Vision for State Park Architecture.

**Heidi Hohmann**, ASLA, is an associate professor of landscape architecture at Iowa State University, where she has taught landscape history and design since 2000. A licensed landscape architect, she previously worked in private and public practice in Minneapolis, Vermont, and Boston, specializing in the preservation of historic landscapes.

Ecologist and author **Cornelia F. Mutel** has written many books on midwestern natural history for lay audiences, including *Fragile Giants: A Natural History of the Loess Hills, The Emerald Horizon: The History of Nature in Iowa, A Watershed Year: Anatomy of the Iowa Floods of 2008*, and *A Sugar Creek Chronicle: Observing Climate Change from a Midwestern Woodland*. Now retired from her position as a senior science writer at IIHR-Hydroscience & Engineering, the University of Iowa, she lives with her husband in an oak woodland near Iowa City and remains active in conservation issues and education.

**John Pearson** is the coauthor of *Deep Nature: Photographs from Iowa* and *The Guide to Iowa's State Preserves*. He holds a master's degree in forestry from Southern Illinois University and a doctorate in botany from the University of Wyoming. From 1982 to 1985, he worked as an ecologist for The Nature Conservancy in South Dakota. Since 1985, he has held the position of ecologist with the Iowa Department of Natural Resources, working with endangered species, the state preserves system, and the environmental review process.

As a research geologist with the Iowa Geological Survey for thirty-eight years, **Jean C. Prior** focused on forecasting the depth and quality of groundwater supplies, the interpretation and protection of significant natural areas in Iowa, and the development of educational materials related to the state's geology and landscape history. She is the former editor of *Iowa Geology,* author of *Landforms of Iowa*, editor of *Iowa: Portrait of the Land*, and lead author of *Iowa's Groundwater Basics.* She served on the State Preserves Advisory Board, is a past president of the Iowa Academy of Science, and contributed to the Iowa Public Television series *Land between Two Rivers.*

After completing graduate studies at the University of Missouri, Columbia, in 1971, **Jim Scheffler** started a thirty-year career with the Iowa Conservation Commission/Iowa Department of Natural Resources. There he held a variety of supervisory and administrative positions, including assistant bureau chief of state parks. His special projects included developing the Iowa Civilian Conservation Corps museum at Backbone State Park and the Maquoketa Caves State Park visitor center. In addition to his many contributions throughout his career, he was considered the resident state park historian.

**William E. Whittaker** is the editor of the *Journal of the Iowa Archeological Society* and editor and coauthor of *Frontier Forts of Iowa: Indians, Traders, and Soldiers, 1682–1862* and *The Archaeological Guide to Iowa.* He is currently the research director for the Iowa Office of the State Archaeologist at the University of Iowa. He has led numerous archaeological surveys and excavations throughout the state during his twenty-five-year career.

# Index of Photographers

Adkins, Lain, 78, 79

Board, Nancy, 188

Boylen, Scott, 6, 244

Brandt, Pamela, 155, 156, 157

Bugalski, Rich, 154

Button, Brian, 167

Byrnes, Mike, 156, 157, 190

Carr, Doug, 66, 67

Chatfield, Glenn, 86

Christensen, Buck, 118

Conrad, Lora, 251

Craig, Don, 116, 142, 144, 154, 160, 186

Curtis, Ben, 122

Eland, Jo, 112, 113

Environmental Law and Policy Center, 58

Formanek, Ken, cover, 55, 124, 150, 210, 214, 215

Gibbs, Brian, 24, 54, 73, 84, 110, 120, 192, 201, 206, 212, 222, 229, 250, 251, 241, 254

Goodfreephotos.com, 45

Hargis, S. C., 178

Hildebrand, John, 74, 216

Iowa Department of Natural Resources, 50, 52, 55, 56, 46, 56, 57, 64, 69, 95, 96, 97, 100, 123, 125, 126, 128, 150, 155, 179, 184

Iowa Geological Survey, 89

Iowa Tourism, 68, 129, 249

Johnson, Ron, 252

Kane, Kevin, 49, 70, 141, 143, 173

Kesse, Vic, 48

Kurtz, Carl, 18, 47, 94, 151, 202, 203, 204, 211, 219, 228, 243

Liechty, Jim, 146, 147

MacBride, Linda, 183

Missouri Department of Conservation, 61

Morphew, Sarah, 82

Pearson, John, 81, 88, 91, 105, 107, 152, 153, 159, 169, 171, 181, 187, 198, 213, 225, 235, 239, 242

Poggensee, Don, 42, 50, 59, 60, 62, 72, 92, 98, 99, 101, 102, 108, 138, 140, 166, 170, 172, 174, 175, 191, 208, 209, 213, 235, 257

Popma, Marlys, 95, 109, 111, 115, 165

Rowley, Erik, 71

Scheffler, Jim, xii, xx, 51, 52, 55, 106, 119, 121, 152, 155, 176, 177, 182

Searles, Leland, 43, 63, 73, 83, 85, 87, 159, 161, 163

Smedes, Ty, 250

Stanski, Joseph, 105

Stone, Larry, 12, 44, 65, 76, 80, 90, 100, 114, 162, 180, 199, 200, 205, 217, 218, 224, 225, 227, 234, 256, 258, 240, 252

Terpstra, Warren, 77, 104, 138, 164, 168, 248, 255

Thompson, Reece, 47, 189

Tschirgi, Matt, 148

Whittaker, William E., 220, 221, 226

PILOT KNOB TOWER
FOREST CITY, IA
37109

CAMPER    WATER'S FINE    DEVILS WAY

PATION POINT    WAUBONSIE STATE PARK, IA    C226

TABLE ROCK
at The Ledges
Des Moines
Fresh Air Home
Between Boone
and Luther, Iowa.

The Blow Out. Lower Palisades, Cedar Rapids, Iowa. 2280 D. U. WILLAMS, PHOTOETTE, BLOOMINGTON, ILL.

BATH HOUSE & CONCESSION BLDG. AHQUABI STATE PARK. INDIANOLA. IA. 5591

Devils Backbone — 1938

The FOS Hitching Rail Crew -- Thank You, Thank you!

ANOTHER PROJECT OF
PAINT IOWA
BEAUTIFUL